GW00724678

GRAND ORIENTAL
HOTELS

Preface
MICHEL DE GRÈCE

———

Text
MARTIN MEADE
JOSEPH FITCHETT
ANTHONY LAWRENCE

———

Art direction and design
MARC WALTER

———

Photo research and captions
CATHERINE DONZEL

———

J.M   Dent & Sons Ltd

First published in Great Britain in 1987 by
J.M. Dent & Sons Ltd
Aldine House, 33 Welbeck Street
London W1M 8LX

British Library Cataloguing-in-Publication
Data
Grand Oriental Hotels from Cairo to
Tokyo, 1800-1939
  1. Hotels, taverns, etc. — Asia — History
  647'.94501   TX910.A6/

ISBN 0-460-04754-X

Printed in Spain by Novograph, Madrid.

Preceding pages: the *Rambagh Palace*,
Jaipur 1987; the central hall of the Umaid
Bhawan, Jodhpur, 1986; and on the frontis-
piece and title page, silverware of the
Continental of Saigon and paraphernalia
sent in by the hotels, during the creation of
this book.

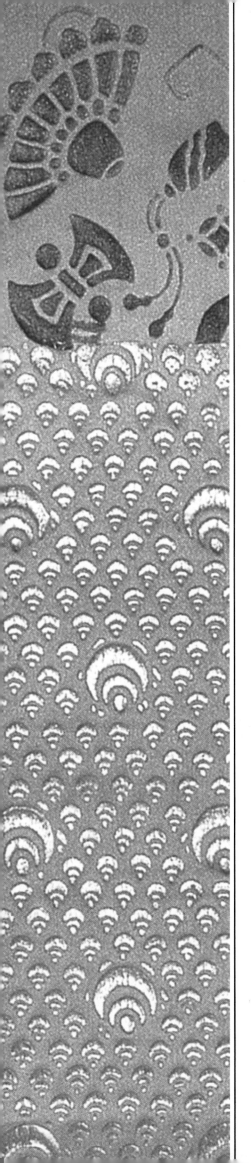
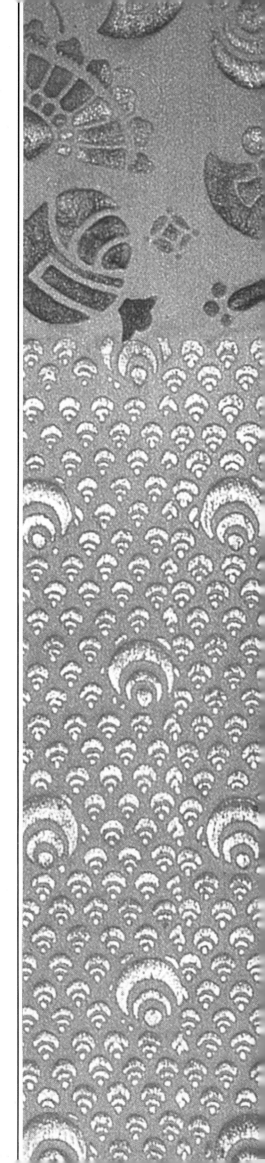

FOREWORD

by Michel de Grèce

P alaces" ... "Orient" .... Few words in the language could be more evocative. Their very mention unleashes a flood of images and desires, a powerful urge to spread one's wings and fly away to the antipodes. I have only to utter them and a dream is set in motion. In my mind's eye, I can see the hotel as the residence of a maharajah. Outside, the heat and incandescent glare of noon. But in the dining room, the closed windows — they are always closed in the Orient, to keep out the heat — create an atmosphere you could cut with a knife. The room, like the palace itself, is enormous, white, a forest of columns. I am the only guest. File upon file of white-draped tables stretch into the distance. There is no sound save the buzzing of flies. At the farthest, darkest end of the room stand two elderly retainers of the palace, now transformed into waiters, wearing emblazoned frock coats and red turbans. Struggling hard against very great drowsiness, they rouse themselves to the prodigious effort of serving my meal, which has long ago become cold.

The food — like the palace — is dated; it tastes of nothing at all, but I don't care. I am spellbound by this atmosphere, in which time seems utterly suspended.

There is no doubt that the great Oriental palaces have lost their lustre. Much of their sumptuous elegance and old world charm have largely disappeared, and their mystery is nearly dead. By definition, the palaces are grand hotels; and today, all over the world, they are tending to become impersonal, dehumanized factories in which the guest is only another number. The service, attention and good food for which one devoutly hopes, and which one has a right to expect for the high prices charged, now seem to be the exclusive province of smaller establishments. As for the Orient, aeroplanes and group travel have brought it within the range of the least adventurous breed of tourist. And yet, despite the slow decay that we call progress, beneath the surface, the Palaces of the Orient still retain a part of their unpredictable quality, their romanticism, and even their glamour.

I belong to a tribe which, unlike other large families, prefers going to hotels rather than to lodging with cousins or friends. Whether they liked it or not, in the past, my relatives have had to move constantly, and as a result, most of them today prefer to live in hotels lock, stock, and barrel; they even tend unconsciously to decorate the interiors of their own homes like hotel bedrooms. Hotels have been in my blood ever since I was a child. The *Minzah* in Tangiers has preserved its great renown over the decades, but for me it has lost the romance I once knew there as a boy during the Second World War. Tangiers at that time was an international city in which representatives and spies of all camps forgathered; and many of these passed through the foyer of the *Minzah*. Here my family alighted en masse. My patriotic parents, uncles and aunts retreated into corners to hold mysterious political meetings. Left to myself, I ordered a succession of exotic dishes which I charged to my grandmother's account, having discovered that her name worked like a charm. Nor was the *Minzah* the only Moroccan hotel we frequented; I became familiar, through my relatives, with many others just as famous though considerably less elegant. Motivated as they were, less by a sense of economy than by loyalty, they used a whole network of hotels — such as the *Balima* in Rabat — which had once been great but had since descended into the pit. In these places my relatives were at ease; they were on first-name terms with all the staff, profited greatly from their kindness, and obtained innumerable special privileges. Best of all, they taught me never to attach too much importance to the presence, or absence, of a three-star rating.

Today, I travel frequently in the Orient; to me, as to many others, the great hotels symbolize the East, just as for the natives they symbolize the West. After all, they were originally designed to receive Western guests and to cater to their needs and customs. But at the time these palaces were built, they were seen to be the embodiment of Western colonialism; hence they became natural targets for local nationalists. In one of the most dramatic epi-

On left
A bell-hop of the *Mamounia,*
Marrakech, 1987.

9

sodes of the struggle for Israeli independence, the Irgun blew up the *King David Hotel* in Jerusalem, a bastion for the British who at that time were occupying the country. A few years later, Egyptian nationalists set fire to *Shepheard's Hotel* in Cairo, from which generations of their British masters had looked arrogantly down upon them.

With the dawn of independence, the great hotels (The *Raffles* in Singapore, the *Mount Lavinia* near Colombo, and many others) underwent a metamorphosis, from being abodes of hated colonialists to repositories of a prestigious past. In almost unimaginable detail, their managements seek to supply every possible necessity that is a copy of the model English day, but little by little indigenous ways have crept into this esoteric code, and the effects on the service are surprising, to say the least. In order to give satisfaction to a Western clientèle, the hotel must adopt every feature of a high tradition that is close to sacrosanct. It is the 24th of December, and we are at the *Cataract Hotel*, Aswan. Outside, the sun's rays may be blinding and the heat intense, but nevertheless it's Christmas. And where the devil can one find a Christmas tree in Nubia? The problem is solved by hanging shreds of cotton as snowflakes to the fronds of a date palm; then, in the great red granite foyer of the hotel (a masterpiece of tropical colonial architecture), Father Christmases are installed; grotesque, but touching in their grotesqueness, amid this decor and sweltering heat.

Before the reader allows himself to be tempted by the living grand hotels pictured and described in this book, perhaps we should pay homage to certain of the genre which have vanished forever. Some fell victim to the combined forces of real estate speculation and corruption. Where, for example, is the Cairo *Semiramis*, that 1880-Louis XVI-Levantine marvel, which sheltered many a distinguished foreigner who had been barred from *Shepheards* by British snobbery? and although it was not in the Orient, I cannot resist mentioning the defunct *Hôtel de Madrid* in Seville, which was anyway thoroughly oriental in aspect and located in a city that remains oriental to the marrow. The *Hôtel de Madrid* was a 19th-century Mossareb-Baroque palace. It had courtyards with fountains, geranium-covered balconies, sooty portraits of hidalgos and black furniture with mouldings. Every room was like the mortuary chamber of a Catholic king. In short, the *Hôtel de Madrid* was a place of enchantment, but despite that, the Franco régime allowed it to be demolished.

Other equally known legendary palaces have been murdered by modernism. Boris, a brawling white Russian, was one of the most conspicuous persons in Nepal. He habitually spent six months of the year in prison, atoning for some peccadillo, where he received all Katmandu in his cell with champagne and caviar. For the other six months, Boris kept a hotel to which the whole world flocked. The place was a vast, run-down fortified palace from the time of the former Rana dynasty. In its gloomy passages hung full-length, jewel-bedecked portraits of the previous owners. The bedrooms seethed with evil spirits and through the courtyards wandered pigs from Boris' sties. At Palmyra, the *Méridien* and other hotel chain palaces have eclipsed *L'Auberge de la Reine Zenobie (Queen Zenobia's Inn)* which not so long ago was the only "modern" building amid the expanse of pink ruins. This hotel was the work and domain of a woman who was almost as famous in her day as Queen Zenobia herself: Countess Margot Dandurain, an adventuress of fabulous stature. Long after she died, veterans would sit up late of a winter night in the hotel's freezing salon (the scene of many an orgy directed by the lady), telling tales of her most scandalous exploits.

Many a haven has been obliterated by politics. What remains of the *Saint-Georges* in Beirut? If this great institution is ever rebuilt on its rock by the sea, will it ever recapture the atmosphere which had made it so utterly unique? In the mellow bar of the *Saint-Georges*, journalists, politicians, dealers, millionaires, informers, courtesans and other celebrities from all over the Middle East were wont to gather. The place epitomized that special ambience of worldliness, frivolity and excitement which used to be the Lebanon. Others of the great hotels stand yet, but changes of régime have turned them into empty shells. Who today would turn aside for a spell at the *Shah Abbas* in Ispahan, that admirable 17th-century caravanserai converted into a luxury hotel? Who would want to stay at that hotel in Tripoli, a vestige of colonialism which until recently was run by Italians just as well as it ever was before the war? And who, finally, will ever revisit the hotel at Angkor, the *L'Auberge des Ruines*, where it stands isolated by the jungle and dominated by tall trees, from which one used to gaze at the prodigious ruins of the great temple in the glow of sunrise or bathed by the light of the moon?

In the Far East, the brand new skyscraper hotels contend so savagely among themselves in point of comfort, luxury and good taste that they are all exactly alike. I cannot distinguish them in my memory. Even the august *Peninsula Hotel* in Hong Kong, despite its brilliant colonial past, has not escaped this rule; if I remember it at all, it is because of the French antique dealer lurking in a shop in the foyer, who waylaid me garrulously every morning with gossip from the hotel and the town.

By contrast, I feel a kind of tenderness for the Bombay *Taj Mahal*, which for me is indelibly associated with my first sight of India. I have fond memories of Eiffel Tower-like steel structures, waves of brightly-coloured, embroidered saris (it was before Mrs Gandhi's sumptuary laws), and exquisite, moist heat. Outside my window was the grey sea, the grey sky, and a huge banyan tree loaded with shrieking birds.

The skyscraper hotels of Delhi, the *Ashoka* and the *Oberoi*, I leave to diplomats (whole embassies are entrenched in them), along with the international conferences and the de luxe group travel organizations. Wise initiates will turn a deaf ear to the recommendations of agencies and will let themselves be guided by travellers more seasoned than themselves, before passing on the information they have gleaned. And in Delhi they will go to the *Imperial*. The Tibetan refugees who twenty years ago stood along the railings selling delectable junk are still there — only now they have become multinationals. Inside, the Indian peddlers still trot at your heels, trickling gems through their fingers, and the red upholstery is still threadbare to the point of decrepitude. Most of the lightbulbs are burned out, but the lamps are delightfully bizarre. Likewise, the bellboys understand nothing at all, yet their philosophical air is irresistible.

After a period of initiation into this folklore, one may gain access to a jealously-guarded secret, the small and marvellous *Claridges Hotel*, which transports its guests instantly and totally to the era of the Raj. Likewise, in Lucknow, it is out of the question to stay at the relatively modern *Clark's Hotel*. The manager here, wishing to assist me in my researches and knowing (or pretending to know) the entire Indian aristocracy, at one stage got his maharajahs confused and sent me to the wrong one. No, at Lucknow the *Carlton* is the place to go: a pure delight, more exotic even than *Claridges* at Delhi. In the deserted suites at the *Carlton*, the Victorian furniture and the bibelots assume grotesque shapes under the great chandeliers, the light of which, once resplendent, is now reduced to a thrifty glow. Behind the moucharabies, the servants stand unseen; to judge by their wandering demeanour, all are reincarnations. Monkeys chatter in the heavy foliage that smothers the verandahs, and one half expects to see a cobra's head rising from the jardinière.

Before I can fully appreciate the soft banality of contemporary three star hotels, I need conditioning. After a week spent crossing the rugged, brigand-infested Madhya Pradesh, utterly submerged in authenticity and dust, it was delicious to arrive at the *Taj View* in Agra, to loll in a suite as sumptuous as that of the Grand Mogul himself, and to meet again with operable plumbing.

Naturally, when I choose my hotels, I am always ready to sacrifice a considerable proportion of comfort to style. But there are limits.

For many years I had put up with a certain celebrated hotel, the glory of Damascus under the mandate, and still, even now, frequented by the best families of Syria. The place was slowly crumbling to the ground, but for the sake of "bon ton" everybody affected not to notice. But one fine day I decided I had had enough of servants who goggled at me and who never registered my messages, and took my custom to the local *Meridien*. It goes without saying that I would never have abandoned the old ship, rotten though she was, had she retained even a particle of charm.

It is possible, and perhaps even diverting, to tolerate extravagant service, but bad service is flatly unbearable, particularly if the bill is astronomical to boot. There is a world-famous grand hotel in Marrakech, with the most enchanting décor one could wish for and fairy-tale gardens; but all these things were set at naught by the offhand manners of the staff, which had reached such an appalling level of nuisance a few years back that one risked a fit of terminal exasperation from one moment to the next. Why, then, would I put up with similar inconvenience at the *Djamal Palace* in Fez? Because here the laziness of the servants was innocent. Instead of systematic ill will, one encountered disorder in its pure form. The dust covering everything merely emphasized the hotel's tarnished splendour; the dense lingering atmosphere of a past filled with colour seemed to be imprisoned within its walls.

There are some grand hotels which deserve a pilgrimage, even though prudence counsels us to avoid staying in them. In Istanbul, for example, I can never resist stopping off at the *Pera Palace*, between visits to my two favourite mosques. This establishment is a triumph of the opulent rococo-1900 style which for some reason blossomed (entirely sui generis) in the territories of the Sultan. Amid the *Pera Palace's* marbles, columns and gilded bronze, standing in front of the magnificent, ante-diluvian elevator, I seem to see the people who came here at the beginning of the century — the stylish drifters and exiles newly arrived on the Orient Express, the elegant, affected men and women who flourished in the perfumed stench of a moribund empire. These images of the past are so palpable at the *Pera Palace* that I rarely linger there for long.

In many of the region's capitals, I prefer Hilton Hotels to all others — for the simple reason that the Middle East has succeeded in corrupting this very competent chain. Every one of the Hiltons seems to have started out "right", that is to say that when they opened they were thoroughly correct, antiseptic, impersonal and totally dull. Then, little by little as the years went by, they acquired pith and character, their ambience grew richer, and heresies emerged to challenge the Word of Conrad Hilton in the form of the splendid eccentricities which are natural to the Orient. My favourite of all the family is the old *Nile Hilton* in Cairo, which I have staunchly supported for more than two decades. This hotel commenced in lamentable style, for in its early years an African diplomat, having decided to stay at the hotel on his wedding night, ate and consumed his bride there, an event which provoked a stir in the world. Sad to say, occidental rigour has now ousted charming local ways. No longer can one slip a modest tip to the concierge, as in the old days, and obtain at a moment's notice as many rooms as one may desire, with the hotel packed out and every bed reserved one year in advance.

From this place, too, I recall many moments when the miraculous sweetness of Egyptians was shown to me. At one time, the telephone system had completely given up the ghost. There was not the faintest hope of obtaining even a Cairo number, let alone abroad; I would have to wait between 8 and 12 hours, and maybe till the next day. But I wept and pleaded with the girl at the switchboard: my poor wife was waiting for my call, she would worry, she would suffer dreadfully ... and within ten minutes I had a line to Paris.

I still cannot decide which view I prefer from the top floors: the one across the slow, eternal waters of the imperial Nile, or the one which surveys the pullulating Minah El Thariz square. But the bulk of my time at the *Nile Hilton* is spent at ground level. I will have nothing to do with the *Belgian Tavern*, incongruously shipped piece by piece from its place of origin to the land of the pharaohs: my preference is for the cafeteria, which is certainly the most amusing cheap restaurant in the country. But the best place for watching people is the foyer, and here, with my insatiable curiosity, I position myself.

The herds of tourists, bright red, sweating, utterly exhausted by the pyramids, have been diverted to the other big hotels, which are much more recent and more heavily advertised, and where nothing would induce me to set foot. The tourists installed at the *Nile Hilton* are so erudite that every one of them looks like a "Herr Professor". Anxious businessmen pace to and fro. Characters of appallingly doubtful aspect hang about, assiduously representing a vanished era of espionage. Guests attending receptions given by members of the new Cairene high society (these receptions nearly all take place on the mezzanine) descend to take the air; one sees women with languid eyes passing in groups of three, buttoned up tight in their lamé dresses and sporting prodigious coiffures. Youyous and tambourines announce a wedding party; the merry participants thread their way between the mountains of suitcases and mingle with the ordinary departures and arrivals. The *Nile Hilton* is like a novel come to life: a novel with the added advantage of having no end.

Certain oriental hotels achieve a magic which is absolute — the *Lake Palace* at Udaipur, for example, with its white marble reflected in water, its cascades of flowers, its fairy-tale apartments, its legends and its voracious crows. But is not the *Lake Palace* a trifle too famous? On the other hand, who, apart from a handful of lucky travellers, knows the *Baron Hotel* at Aleppo; in fact, who even goes to Aleppo, the least commercialized city in the Levant, the richest in unsuspected marvels, and the only one where the past is completely integrated with the present. The *Baron* was built during the Ottoman Empire at a time when, under the pretext of rummaging around in the desert, archaeologists were vying with each other as spies. Lawrence of Arabia stayed at the *Baron* after taking part in a British archaeological expedition and his bills may still be seen there, mysteriously "paid by Madame X". Max Mallowan, another archaeologist, was staying at the *Baron* with his wife Agatha Christie at the same time and malicious tongues proclaimed that a liaison between the hero and the lady novelist had occurred in the hotel. Many travellers, kings, and representatives of the world's governments, have passed through here. But today the place is a haunt of phantoms, because the main flow of the clientèle has been diverted. The ghosts are now expelling the last habitués, and soon they will be the only occupants of the *Baron Hotel*. The swart, aged, rickety chambermaids speak no known language; like the musically-named proprietor, Coco Masmoulian, they are Armenian. Mr Masmoulian is married to an English lady and serves tea in surroundings that are even more British than the real thing. In the corridors, one or two fine pieces of furniture float above the wreckage, but the darkness is so opaque that one is more likely to bump into them than admire them. The floorboards undulate capriciously, none of the wardrobe doors can be induced to close, the taps emit hideous groans and no one in living memory has ventured to taste the hotel's food. What is it, then, that makes the *Baron Hotel* so truly, unforgettably poetic, that makes everyone who has been there speak of it with deep emotion? I don't know. Nor do I know why I myself think of the place with such profound nostalgia. Early in the morning come the sounds that are so uniquely oriental, so clear and distinct from one another and from the background rumble of the already busy city; these sounds enter the open window, along with the first heat of the day. The peeling shutters admit a soft light during the hour of siesta, washing the room with gold; a hotel bedroom, whose very banality is a trick of the imagination. Then it is time for the ritual aperitif, when a semblance of coolness returns to Aleppo ... and this aperitif, which is raki, the least pernicious of the hotel's offerings, is taken on the upper terrace, whilst one surveys the obsessive movement of the street below, and saturates one's consciousness with sounds, colours and images. For me, the *Baron* epitomizes everything I seek in the great hotels of the Orient. It offers both the sensation of being in a far country, and the sensation of otherworldliness that exists only in places that possess their own deep and inveterate character.

GRAND HOTELS AND PALACES THE DIMENSIONS OF A DREAM

by Martin Meade

The *Grand Hotel de l'Oasis* and the *Aletti* in Algiers, the *Pera Palace*. in Istanbul, *Shepheard's* and the *Gezira Palace* in Cairo, the *Taj* in Bombay, the *Oriental* in Bangkok, the *Eastern and Oriental* in Penang, the *Raffles* in Singapore, the *Peninsula* in Hong Kong and the *Manila* in the Philippines — this cavalcade of caravanserai-palaces with such evocative names, stretching from the Mediterranean to Japan and to the Americas on the other side, marks the staging posts in the great colonial and commercial adventure that spanned the globe. But it also represents the embodiment of a popular taste for "orientalism", which had inspired a European ethnocentric artistic and literary fantasy since the 19th century, and brought in its wake that new phenomenon, the tourist enthralled by the exotic Orient — provided such could be enjoyed in the comfortable surroundings of a Grand Hotel of the kind already so familiar in Europe and America.

Despite the concession to climate provided by the verandah and shaded loggias, the Grand Hotels of the Orient, however eclectic, were rarely cut off from their European origins. They all share that hallmark always intrinsic to their design — the transposition and adaptation of their architecture, to the new scale of their specific location, to the climate and materials of the country and culture which they imposed themselves upon and with which, to some extent, they were integrated. It is this very peculiar mixture of the exotic and the familiar that endows the Grand Hotels of the Orient with their special character, interest and attraction.

BIRTH OF THE GRAND ORIENTAL HOTELS

Among the new types of building to appear in the first half of the 19th century to meet the needs of economic and social expansion in American and European industrial towns and cities, the Grand Hotel was one of the most notable innovations. There is a direct correlation between the evolution of the hotel and the development of public transport during the industrial revolution: it was the introduction of the railways that proved to be so decisive in the institution of the Grand Hotel, both as a viable commercial venture and as an essential social facility — and hence a key symbol for the new "urbane" middle classes' progressive aspirations. From 1840 onwards in Britain and in France — and later elsewhere — a hotel for travellers became the indispensable neighbour to the railway station. With the building of main line terminus stations in city centres, these two building types could be

13

Excerpt from a brochure
of the *Dollar Steamship Line,*

combined, as was the case with the *Great Western Hotel* and Paddington Station in London (1852–54).

The Grand Hotel was an American invention (the first was the *City Hotel* in New York, built in 1794-95 to designs by Benjamin Latrobe). But it was soon to make its appearance in monarchist Europe and bring with it a radical change of lifestyle: travel ceased to be a hardship. It became a pleasure, then an escape from the ordinary and the humdrum, which the hotel-palace — far from being merely functional — did so much to enhance.

The railway network and, with it, the Grand Hotel, gradually expanded beyond Europe and round the Mediterranean. With the inauguration of the Paris-Istanbul line came the celebrated "Orient Express" (1884), a train which the Compagnie Internationale des Wagons-Lits (CIWL) fitted out as luxuriously as a Grand Hotel. As a logical outcome the CIWL set up its own international hotel chain, (the first of its kind) to provide its passengers with hotel accommodation that was as comfortable as its trains. The "Grand Hotel des Wagons-Lits" made its appearance at Nice, Monte-Carlo, Lisbon, Brindisi (a major port of embarkation for the Orient), at Cairo and even, briefly in 1904, in Peking.

This "Belle Epoque" of oriental travel was heralded by the opening of the Suez Canal, which was inaugurated with great pomp in 1869. Thereafter, the liner — that other great invention of the steam age — would take over from the railways. Before long, the spread of major commercial shipping routes and colonial expansion were followed by the Grand Hotel all the way to the Far East. In the opulent manner of the Orient Express, the great liners of the P & O, the Messageries Maritimes and the Lloyd-Triestino companies in their turn became floating palaces. Colonial officers and businessmen felt as at home on these ships as they did on the verandah or at the bar of *Shepheard's* in Cairo, the *Taj* in Bombay, or the *Raffles* in Singapore. And

French and British officials in Ismailia celebrating the opening of the Suez Canal.

such liners provided tourists with a foretaste of the comforts they were to enjoy at the Grand Hotels while giving full rein to their oriental fantasies.

The era of industrial revolution coincided with that of colonial imperialism. European settlement expanded, encouraged by the boom in commerce as vast tropical territories were exploited to supply new industries. And the growth of commerce gave birth to the Oriental hotel. It was the British Empire that took the lion's share in this colonial epic, which was filled with economic and national rivalry. After the American Declaration of Independence in 1778, British colonialism expanded in the Orient, with India as its focal point. The East India Company had been established there for over a century. Thanks to the farsighted vision of exceptional governor-generals, the Company overtook its Dutch and French rivals and, by the beginning of the 19th century, had consolidated its economic, political and military empire in the sub-continent. The great trading ports of Bombay, Madras and Calcutta were the bridgeheads for a very lucrative trade, both with the hinterland and with China, particularly in tea and Indian opium. The resurgence of a French threat during the Revolutionary and Napoleonic wars encouraged the expansionist policies of governor-generals such as Lord Wellesley (1799-1804). But it was always the demands of commerce — reflected in its ever-growing merchant navy — which prompted the British to establish new trading posts in the Orient, as well as naval bases to protect their shipping routes. And it was in these trading posts that the first Oriental hotels appeared.

Penang was established in Malaysia as early as 1786 to control the Straits of Malacca which lay on the route to China, and this strategic control was further reinforced by the founding of Singapore by Stamford Raffles in 1819. The colonization of the peninsula continued after 1824. Earlier, in 1796, the British had taken Ceylon (Sri Lanka) a Dutch colony. The Dutch, who were then allied with the French were legitimate enemies of Britain, but they were to retain their possessions in the "Spice Islands", now Indonesia. Between 1824 and 1826 the British imposed their presence on Burma and, after the 1840-42 Opium War with China, Britain also gained a permanent trade base in Hong Kong, and five Chinese ports including Shanghai, were opened up to trade with Europe.

European enclaves were set up in China, each with its own western-style hotel, and with the opening of American and Japanese bases after 1890, these hotels further evolved and developed. Spurred by its traditional rivalry with Britain, France expanded her colonialism in North and West Africa as of 1830, and spread her influence to Palestine, Syria and Lebanon. French interests in Egypt prompted the building of the Suez Canal, a major investment in the country's modernization under the reign of the Viceroy Ismail Pasha

Cover of a tourist brochure, 1930s.

(1863-79). A major French presence in the Far East was achieved by the colonization of Indochina, between 1858 and 1893. Each of these stages of French colonization was marked by the building of hotels.

This survey of oriental colonial history and the great exotic travel routes, which brought tourism in their wake, would be incomplete without reference to a very particular development in the beliefs of the British Empire, "on which the sun never set". They were based on the philosophy of imperial destiny, as first postulated by Thomas Carlyle and Sir Charles Dilke, and later eulogized by Kipling — the God-given, civilizing duty of Great Britain, as the "chosen nation", to take up "the white man's burden". It was in this context that the Grand Hotels of the Orient, like other public monuments of the British Empire, took on a very important symbolic value. They, like the Club, represented a place of refuge and of escape, where the "white man" could put down his "burden" for a few moments and savour "the refinements and luxuries of European society" in the company of his own kind.

INDIA:

THE BUNGALOW AS A MODEL

The flourishing of the British Raj in India at the beginning of the 19th century provided seemingly ideal conditions for the growth of the hotel industry on the European model. Yet initially, hotels remained as modest as they were rare in India. On one hand it had long been the East India Company's custom to have bungalows built to house its military, administrative or trading staff during their up-country tours of duty (a practice continued by the present Indian Republic, which still makes use of the facilities built for the Raj). On the other hand, young company clerks based in Bombay, Madras or Calcutta were generally accommodated in lodgings and boarding houses which served as residential hotels. A third building type specially tailored to the needs of young bachelors — whether civil or military — posted up-country was the

Excerpt from a Dutch tourist brochure, 1930s.

"chummery", a bungalow built with communal mess facilities and intended for several young officers to share. The widespread provision of these types of residential accommodation — together with the institution of "the Club", a social focus and a masculine haven of leisure — largely explains the initial rarity of the hotel *per se* in India. Outside the three great trading cities, the basic architectural type was the bungalow. Derived from the traditional Bengali mud hut or *bangla* — with overhanging eaves, supported as necessary on posts, to provide shady verandahs — the Anglo-Indian bungalow was a reinterpretation of this indigenous building type to which a Western classical vocabulary was applied. The verandah was treated either as an arcade or as a colonnade. In hot, arid regions where the monsoon was limited, cornices, entablatures and roof terraces were sometimes substituted for pitched roofs. In an elegant adaptation of the English Palladian style to the Indian climate, the classical orders of architecture were applied to the colonnaded verandah (but with a marked and economical preference for the Doric) to provide practical embellishment to a villa type which proved equally suitable for the town, the suburb and the country. The type was established by the end of the 18th century. As designed by the Company's civil and military engineers (who played the role of architect in the colonies until the end of the 19th century), the Anglo-Indian bungalow proved to be a form of architectural typology perfectly adaptable to virtually the entire range of civil and military building, from the governor's residence

The "Chummery" in Jubbulpore: a type of lodging which preceded the construction of hotels in India.

or the officer's or planter's villa to the military mess, the police station, the bank, the club, the chummery or, even, the hotel.

Agra is conveniently located on the Grand Trunk Road, that strategic highway of Mogul origin which the British

Façades of the *Laurie's Hotel,* Agra, 1930s.

restored as the essential backbone of their control over northern India, linking Calcutta to Delhi and the north-west and extending south-west to Bombay. But while Agra was a military and civil station of some considerable importance on this axis, doubtless the main reason for opening an hotel, there was the demand created by the nascent species of the tourist in India, attracted by Agra's famous Mogul monuments, the Taj Mahal and the Red Fort. *Laurie's Hotel*, in Agra, was built in 1854 and is one of the oldest hotels in India (and in the East). Its original character is well-preserved and provides a perfect illustration of the typological flexibility of the Anglo-Indian bungalow. Essentially a horizontal composition of only one storey, generously spread about a quadrangle plan, *Laurie's Hotel* is set in a large compound of garden tended with all the traditional skills of Indian gardeners who have managed, despite the climate, to create lawns to (almost) English standard, exotically juxtaposed with local flowers and trees. In line with the type and with the neo-classical taste of its period, the hotel elevations were set behind a Tuscan colonnade forming a deep verandah reached by a few steps. This verandah, which reads as a continuous screen, was run right round the building, to its full height (the west wing was a later addition, built to match the original). As was customary for all buildings of any pretension of the period, the main entrance took the form of a projecting portico, which had the practical advantage of affording the clientèle protection from the scorching sun, or the monsoon rains, as they got in or out of their carriages. (The internal arrangements took the typical bungalow form, as adapted to an appropriately enlarged scale. The principal public rooms were located centrally, so as to receive most of their daylight indirectly, from the verandah. However, these rooms were designed to rise above the roof terrace, so clerestory windows were incorporated at high level, letting in only oblique light (filtered as necessary with blinds) while also providing good ventilation in the rooms. The bedrooms were arranged around the perimeter of the building and opened directly onto the verandah. Each had French windows protected by louvred shutters. Because of the climatic conditions, French windows were generally the only source of daylight in the bedrooms, which were also provided with a vent at high level, below the ceiling. The beds were always furnished with mosquito-nets and each bedroom had its own bathroom sometimes entered via an *en suite* dressing room. Bathroom fittings long remained minimal but effective: at best a plain zinc-bath tub (sometimes only a water pitcher) and the closet. There were no taps, water for washing being brought by servants who had direct access to the bathrooms from a service gallery. "Night soil" was also discreetly removed from the closets by servants. Whenever possible, windows and doors were aligned to create through-draughts, but the heat was such that all rooms were furnished with *punkahs*, following Indian custom. These consisted of sheets of materials or canvas, hung from the ceiling and pulled to and fro, to create a breeze by means of a cord, operated by a *punkah wallah* posted outside the room. This simple manual device was superseded in the 20th century by electric fans which are still known as *punkahs*. Victorian

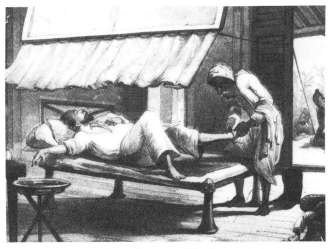

The *punkah* and, on the verandah, the *punkah wallah*, India, 1860s.

ingenuity also devised mechanical means of cooling air: vast bellows operated by teams of servants, to blow air into the building over blocks of ice; and the "thermantidote" — a fan driven by servants or by oxen, to force air through water-sodden blinds. As an additional precaution against the climate in the hot weather, traditional Indian screens or "tatties" of plaited grass were hung outside the building, between the verandah columns, and regularly doused with water. Other than the columns and pilasters of the reception rooms, the interior decoration of *Laurie's Hotel* remained very plain, like so many other hotels of its type. But the soaring height of its ceilings, its very open plan and

Concert at the "club house" in Singapore, c. 1900. The club, like the European-style grand hotel, was, above all, the refuge and safe-keeper of Western values.

the long perspective views along its verandah colonnades endowed it with great classical dignity. The furnishings and facilities were originally very simple and, until the end of the 19th century, visitors were commonly expected to bring their own bed linen to *Laurie's*, as they were also to do in many other hotels in the East, which were sometimes not even equipped with mattresses.

DELHI:

DEVELOPMENT OF THE GRAND HOTELS

Maiden's Hotel, in Delhi, opened virtually at the same time as *Laurie's* in Agra and in the late 1850s and 1860s more European-inspired hotels followed suit, such as *Flashman's* at Rawalpindi, *Faletti's* at Lahore or *Percy's* at Secunderabad. In the light of this essentially mid-century development, it is not surprising that *Spence's Hotel* — opened in 1830 in Wellesley Place, Calcutta — could, with justifiable pride, lay claim to be "The Oldest in Asia".

Lounge of the *Laurie's Hotel,* Agra, c. 1920.

Calcutta was after all the administrative and social hub of the empire, the seat of the Governor General and, during this period, the major business centre and port. Wellesley Place was cut through as a new street circa 1828, opening up the perspective of Government House on the axis of Dalhousie Square. *Spence's Hotel*, sited on the west side of the street, therefore had a highly advantageous position at the heart of the city of white stucco palaces.

Maiden's Hotel and the *Cecil* in Delhi are near mid-19th century contemporaries of *Laurie's* at Agra. The Mogul and earlier Sultanate monuments of the city held as much attraction as those of Agra but, after the 1857 Mutiny and British siege of the city, Delhi was equally frequented for the evocative memories and memorials of these sanguinary events. The proclamation of Queen Victoria as Empress of India at the Imperial Durbar of 1877 in Delhi, followed by the Coronation Durbar of 1903 and that of 1911 at which King George V momentously announced the transfer of the capital from Calcutta to Delhi, all successively enhanced the city's importance and led both hotels to be extended and enlarged.

The *Great Eastern Hotel* in the same prime central area of Delhi, on Court House Street, was in the 1850s being developed by David Wilson as a far more imposing and genuinely "grand" affair. It opened in 1851 as the *Auckland Hotel* and "Hall of All the Nations" but, as with so many other Oriental hostelleries, was also known as *Wilson's Hotel* after its developer. It became known as the *Great*

Façade of the *Percy's,* Secunderabad.

Eastern around 1860, possibly in expectation of the sea route around the Cape taken by I.K. Brunel's "Great Eastern" steam, but more likely the change of name coincided with Wilson's selling out in part to a new hotel company in 1865. The *Great Eastern* acquired those external decorative features characteristic of so many late 19th-century Oriental hotels.

Internally too, the *Great Eastern* was already in the "grand" category of its European contemporaries and, with its 300 bedrooms it certainly appears to have been the first hotel on this scale in the Orient. There was a vast ballroom, probably David Wilson's "Hall of All the

Façade of the *Great Eastern,* Calcutta, 1880.

Nations" and an equally grandiose top-lit dining room and staircase. Until the 1880s, however, only the main bedrooms had the type of bathroom at *Laurie's* in Agra. Running water was then introduced, followed in the 1890s by electric lighting and after the turn of the century, hydraulic lifts; and between the wars the *Great Eastern* was the first place in Calcutta to have air-conditioning installed.

Entrance of the *Cecil Hotel,* Delhi, c. 1930.

BOMBAY:

THE PALATIAL AND THE MONUMENTAL

Bombay, by 1864, had become a booming commercial and industrial centre, a clearing house for the thriving Indian cotton industry which, following on the declining export of American cotton due to the Civil War, now met the voracious needs of the Lancashire mills. The *Great Western Hotel* in Apollo Street, probably opened around 1860, was an early example of a European-scale hotel, not as imposing as Calcutta's *Great Eastern*, but with its dignified

Façade of the *Majestic Hotel,* Bombay, c. 1920

Doric-columned *porte cochère* marking the centre of the 12-bay symmetrical stucco elevation not unlike the Cairo hotels of the same period, with distinctive *jhimils* on wooden hoods shading the windows.

The opening of *Watson's Hotel* in 1867 on Esplanade Road marked the introduction of the large-scale European or American hotel type of the period. *Watson's* (now known as Esplanade Mansions and used as offices) was also innovatory in its construction, being the first iron-framed building in Bombay. *Watson's* screened verandah facade type was subsequently used for more modest Bombay establishments such as the *Byculla Hotel* circa 1870 (opposite the Victoria Museum and Gardens), where the screens are completely flush with the verandah fronts, creating a "curtain wall" that is sheltered from monsoon

Façade of the *Great Western Hotel,* Bombay, c. 1900.

rains by the projecting eaves of the roof. In the 1890s *Green's Hotel* (originally built as mansion flats) situated near Apollo Bunder and *Watson's*, provided an interesting development of the type. The effect was of a number of bungalows piled one on top of the other and gave the elevations a striking, pagoda-like appearence.

By the early 1890s, a major civic improvement programme had produced a magnificent series of High Victorian public buildings in Bombay, commensurate with the city's commercial prestige. Initially designed in a bold Venetian Gothic style well adapted to the climate, these buildings increasingly incorporated Indo-Saracenic features. Their influence is reflected in the contemporary *Majestic Hotel*, with its lively display of minarets and loggias freely derived from the Sultanate architecture of Ahmadabad.

The most spectacular Bombay hotel in this vein is the great *Taj Hotel* of 1904. Commanding superb views over Bombay harbour from Apollo Bunder, by the triumphal arch of the "Gateway to India", this towering imposingly-domed "palace" immediately attracted the attention of the tourist as he arrived on a luxurious P&O liner. The *Taj* was designed by the local English architect, W. Chambers, for

Façade of the *Watson's,* Bombay, 1895.

the great Parsee industrialist Jamsetgi N. Tata who, in the 1880s, conceived the idea of providing Bombay with a Grand Hotel fitted out to the most advanced international standards. Completed at a cost of £500,000 the hotel had its own steam laundry, aerated bottling plant, electroplating facilities for its silverware, a Nora silver burnishing machine, a crockery washing plant, a telegraph service, electric lighting, and of course, lifts. Originally the main entrance for ease of carriage traffic was via Esplanade Road, and a large forecourt garden between the wings allowed more bedrooms to be given the advantage of the sea view and the westerly breezes. Chambers dressed his symmetrical elevations to catch the eye with a wonderful eclectic profusion of Gujerati, Romanesque, Gothic, Renaissance and even Swiss chalet ornamentation. The interiors had a similar exotic blend of Indo-Saracenic and European styles, of which the grand staircase, rising with spectacular flying flights beneath the great dome, and the ballroom are the best preserved examples. In the wings, the bedrooms follow the Anglo-Indian hotel tradition in that they give on to open balustraded galleries arranged around a succession of internal sky-lit courts.

Façade of the *Green's Hotel,* Bombay, c. 1900.

Recognized from the beginning as one of the world's great hotels and a potent symbol of the grandeur of the British Raj, the *Taj* in the hallowed company of *Shepheard's* in Cairo, the *Raffles* in Singapore, and the *Peninsula* in Hong Kong, stands as a palatial monument to the imperial heyday of the oriental hotel.

FRENCH NORTH AFRICA:

A STYLISTIC INTEGRATION

The assimilation of indigenous styles that evolved out of orientalist romanticism and an eclectic taste for the Mauresque, was to find an echo in the hotel architecture of French North Africa, where an imperial policy of greater integration was developing, informed by a more widespread appreciation of Arab civilization which colonial and decorative arts exhibitions served to foster.

The *Hotel Saint-George* , opened in 1912 on the heights above Algiers is an impressive exercise in North Africa vernacular revival. It is set in large gardens with cloistered, fountain-embellished patios. Lavish interiors with Maghrebine plaster and tilework and arcades are complemented on the exterior by cantilevered balconies and loggias and a lively polychrome variety of local building materials. This

The *Transatlantique* in Bou Saada, 1980s.

is no mere pastiche but rather a reflection of contemporary regionalist, rationalist and late *Art Nouveau* trends in French architecture. In Morocco, under the enlightened aegis of Marechal Lyautey's Protectorate, a particularly sensitive contemporary reinterpretation of the Maghrebine architectural tradition was developed by architect-planner Henri Prost, assisted amongst others by A. Laprade, J. Marrast, A. Marchiso. The Grand Hotel *Tour Hassan* (circa 1918–20) in Prost's new garden city development of Rabat, and the *Mamounia* at Marrakech, designed by Prost and Marchiso which opened in 1923, have cool, simple, white or ochre-washed surfaces with restrained,

EGYPT:

PALACES BY THE NILE

For the traveller romantically enthralled by the Orient, Egypt — with the Great Sphinx, the Pyramids and all the other monumental marvels of Antiquity and Islam strewn across the desert sands or along the legendary banks of the Nile — exerted a most powerful attraction, and with the coming of the steam age became much more accessible. The first railway line linking the new port facilities at Alexandria with Cairo was completed in 1857 and the line

The seafront boulevard in Algiers and, on the left, the *Hôtel Terminus et de l'Europe*

already modernist, transposition of traditional decorative forms. These are typically fine examples of this avant-garde school. But sadly, the *Mamounia* has been entirely recast in pseudo-Moroccan style. The match reveals the close affinities and influence this architecture "in the Arab manner" had on the evolution of Art Deco and the Modern Movement, aspects of which become more evident in such 1930s hotels as the *Aletti* in Algiers or the *Transatlantique* at Ban Saada. The popularity of this "Arab style" had already been confirmed by the early 1920s with its adoption by the Compagnie Générale Transatlantique for the chain of hotels built throughout French North Africa.

was extended to Suez by 1859, while de Lesseps' great canal, built as a joint Franco-Egyptian venture, finally opened ten years later. In parallel with these innovations in transport, Cairo was rapidly developed westwards to the Nile and Gezira, with a fashionable residential and business district planned on Parisian lines. This "new" town centre naturally became the favoured location for European-style hotels catering to an increasingly cosmopolitan and demanding clientèle.

Earliest and most famous of these establishments was *Shepheard's Hotel* which opened as early as 1841 in a converted house which had served as Napoleon's head-quarter during the Egyptian campaign. It was located just outside the old city walls on what was to become Ezbekiyah Boulevard or, as it is now known, El-Gumhuriyya Street. The hotel's founder, Mr Shepheard, owned a company called Preston Capes but enterprisingly judged the hotel trade in Cairo to be a more lucrative line of business. Such was the hotel's popularity as an essential port of call for all those travelling to or returning from India and the Far East, that a major rebuilding programme was completed in 1891 with yet further extensions made in 1899, 1904, 1909 and 1927; the venerable building was finally demolished after fire damage in 1957.

Before the rebuilding of 1891, *Shepheard's* had acquired conventional mid-19th century stucco elevations with a few simple Italianate classical details, balustraded balconies and a columned verandah porch. Apart from Venetian blinds supplemented by exotically patterned awnings to keep out the sun, there was little to distinguish its architecture from its European precedent. But *Shepheard's* best known feature was its delicate cast ironwork verandah erected in 1891 in front of the entrance to the main block and extending on a terrace on either side. With its rattan tables and chairs, palms and patterned

Other European-style hotels soon joined *Shepheard's*, on or off the Ezbekiyah boulevard, catering to the increasing number of tourists, who by then, included Americans as well as Europeans.

The *Bristol Hotel*, fairly similar in style to *Shepheard's* though more coarsely detailed, opened under that name in 1875 but appears to date from the 50s. The *Continental*, of the 1860s, was a dignified Italianate classical design with a prominent and imposing portico-porch. These early hotels were rather more English than French in appearance and perpetuated the club or town house image of earlier British hotels. The *Grand Hotel Royal*, however — on the opposite side of the boulevard from *Shepheard's* and dating from the late 1860s — proudly proclaimed itself "le seul hôtel français de premier ordre au Caire" and, not surprisingly, adopted a distinctly French style with ground floor arcade and long balconies. In keeping, too, with the sophisticated reputation of French hôtellerie and the facilities offered by its Spa resort counterparts at Vittel or Vichy, the *Grand Hotel Royal* provided hydrotherapy baths and showers for the benefit of the guests, as well as the reading, reception and smoking rooms found in the other European Cairo establishments.

Façade of the *Grand Hotel,* Calcutta, c. 1910.

awnings, it was cosmopolitan Cairo's social hub. Here, and on less august hotel verandahs, the western tourist watching the "teeming flow of Islamic life" became according to Edouard Schure in his 1898 *Sanctuaries of Orient* "fatally orientalized ... spending whole days in wonder before the stream of passersby in a state of beatitude similar to that induced by Kif."

Under the vigorous policy of Khedive Ismail however, a new Cairo had rapidly developed as of 1867 with the aid of French town planners and engineers. The road on the western fringe of the old city in which *Shepheard's* was situated became the Ezbekiyah boulevard, the main north-south artery of the new town linking the new railway station with the Abdin Palace. At its mid-point, just south of *Shepheard's* the Ezbekiyah Gardens were laid out in 1867, followed by the Opera House opened in 1869 to coincide with the festivities marking the inauguration of the Suez Canal.

The *Grand Continental Hotel* (now the *Continental Savoy*) facing the Ezbekiyah Gardens and the newly completed Opera temporarily eclipsed even *Shepheard's* senior status and prestige by its grander scale and its 150-bedrooms. Built with a projecting entrance and deep wings allowing cross-ventilation, the *Grand Continental's* design pragmatically combined contemporary French rationalist planning and eclectic stylistic trends in architecture. The hotel's hybrid veneer of debased classical and Renaissance decorative detail was originally picked out in white on a dark background, giving the façade a livelier, more exotic character than it now has. But a suitably orientalizing addition of the period still survives in the Mauresque canopy over the steps of the main entrance. The *Heliopolis Palace Hotel*, on the north-eastern outskirts of Cairo, offers an early example of the use of indigenous traditional styles in the Middle East. This vast "palace" integrated in the plan of the model garden city of

Garden verandah of the *Luxor Hotel,* Luxor, c. 1930.

Heliopolis was conceived in 1906 by the enlightened Belgian developer Baron Empain, who commissioned E.Jaspar as architect for the hotel, which opened in 1909. Consistent with Baron's design policy for his new town, the hotel's architectural decoration, both inside and out, is a most effective and well adapted revival of the late Mamelouk and Ottoman styles of architecture in Cairo.

Another magnificent hotel, the *Gezira Palace*, was built by Ismail Pasha to receive the Empress Eugénie for the inauguration of the Suez Canal in 1869. The vast expenditure for this event led to an increasingly serious state of the Khedive's finances which were inextricably tied up with those of the State. Hence, the Compagnie Internationale des Wagon-Lits took over the *Gezira Palace* as part of the international chain of hotels they were establishing in the 1890s. The French *Gezira Palace* was possibly designed by Alfred Chapon, architect of the Compagnie de Suez, and had to be erected in the space of a few months to be ready for the Canal's inauguration. This no doubt accounts for the slightly monotonous, mechanical handling of the long elevations — not unlike the cast iron exhibition structures which had impressed Ismail Pasha in Paris two years previously. Indeed extensive use was made of cast iron in the palace's construction. French orientalist taste of the

Façade of the *Winter Palace,* Luxor, c. 1910.

1860s and the Khedive's national pride required that the palace's oriental setting should be reflected in the decorative dressing of the otherwise rationally composed lines of the facades. Mauresque patterns and features, eclectically derived from the traditional architecture of Moorish Spain and Turkey as much as Islamic Egypt, were therefore applied to doorways, windows and cornices, but were most evident in the *moucharabiyeh*-style ironwork of the verandah porches as well as a whole sequence of cast iron and plaster-work garden pavilions, most of which have now disappeared.

The interiors of this royal guest palace were laid out around atrium-like courts, with vast salons, suites and axial marble paved corridors, which proved easily adaptable to Grand Hotel use. This is an early instance of a type of conversion recently adopted for the princely palaces of India. Luxuriously appointed for Eugénie's benefit, the

The *Continental (Grand Continental),* Cairo, c. 1900.

decoration and furnishings of the palace exotically married neo-Louis XV and Louis XVI styles with the Mauresque, the latter notably displayed in the detailing of the corridor perspectives and more eclectically, in the spectacular imperial staircase.

By the 1870s the first hotels had been built at Luxor and Aswan in response to the increasing numbers of serious-minded tourists who desired to pursue their discovery of ancient Egypt and the Nile beyond Cairo and the Pyramids to the temple and city sites of Upper Egypt. The original *Savoy Hotel* and *Luxor Hotel* at Luxor were followed by the *Cataract Hotel* at Aswan; understandably, they were modest affairs very similar to the early Cairo hotels, though making more extensive use of verandahs and loggias due to their open and exposed sites on the edge of the desert. The *Luxor Hotel* had an arcaded ground floor to the entrance front of slightly vernacular Egyptian conformation, in contrast with the conventional European-style shuttered windows and iron balconies of its upper floor. This oriental detail may have been introduced however in the 1920s, when the garden front was "Egyptianized" with a horseshoe-arched verandah. The *Cataract* at Aswan was also altered and enlarged at this time, in an Art Deco streamlined classical style, while the hotel's new dining room was erected as a garden pavilion in the form of a domed mosque in similar style.

By the end of the first decade of this century the aptly named *Winter Palace Hotel* at Luxor had spread on the Nile its imposing classically proportioned edifice overlaid with stylized Egyptian motifs. Raised on a vast balustraded and arcaded terrace sweeping into the grand double staircase and monumental porch, the hotel commands a splendid view of the river; the palatial scale and vast gardens of the *Winter Palace* were only matched in Cairo itself at this date by the *Gezira Palace Hotel.*

The *Pera Palace,* Istanbul, c. 1900.

THE MIDDLE EAST:

CARAVANSERAI AND ORIENT EXPRESS

One of the earliest hotels for western travellers in the Middle East was the *Grand Hotel Bassoul* at Beirut, which probably opened in the 1860s or early '70s when, under pressure from the European powers, the Ottoman Empire and the Levant had become more easily accessible to Westerners. The hotel was built in the manner of Levantine houses with thick stone walls, lofty ceilings and circular clerestory vents to cool the interiors. Its centralized courtyard plan remained faithful to the eastern tradition of the caravanserai. The main accommodation was thus on the first floor with bedrooms leading directly off the landing and the *salon*. This room had triple-arcaded windows in the vernacular style overlooking the sea and was decorated and furnished with a delightfully pragmatic blend of European and Levantine features.

Until well after the turn of the century most Levantine hotels were relatively modest establishments, similar to the *Bassoul*, though the *Parc Hotel* at Jaffa (the port of arrival for tourists to the Holy Land) and the slightly later (1902) *Baron Hotel* at Aleppo, were more sophisticatedly European in their design and facilities. In 1900, the pioneer of organized tour companies in the Orient, Thomas Cook's, was still describing the three-storeyed *Grand New Hotel* in Jerusalem (built in the 1850s with a classical facade to match its pretensions) as the only hotel "in or near Jerusalem with modern water sanitary arrangements."

The comfortable, well-appointed premises of the *American Colony* in Jerusalem were opened as a hotel in 1902, but with its fine vaulted main rooms ranged around a courtyard garden overlooked by high arched windows,

this is a traditional, rather than a purpose-designed hotel. The *Pera Palace* in Istanbul was opened in 1892 by the Compagnie des Wagons-Lits as the necessary luxurious complement to the *Orient Express.* It was in the full-blown multi-storey Grand Hotel style of the French Riviera, complete with heavily-draped and amply-furnished salons, a large, chandelier-hung dining room, billiard room, smoking-room, lifts, etc. Only the reading room gave a slight hint of the Eastern context of this grand hotel where Proust stayed and where Agatha Christie wrote *Murder on the Orient Express.* The *Splendid Palace Hotel* at Buyükada, Istanbul, likewise displays all the characteristics of a contemporary Parisian or Riviera hotel, with pointed domes surmounting the corners of the main facade and balustraded terrace leading down to the banks of the Bosphorous.

SRI LANKA (CEYLON):

RESORT HOTELS

Besides the large urban hotels on the main tourist circuit, there is another type of hotel which caters specifically to travellers who are attracted by the natural charms of the region which they come across. Whether in the hill station resorts of the Nilgiris and the Himalayas (notably in Ootacamund and Simla), in the plains or, later, on the coast in such a delightful-named resort as *Gopalpur-on-sea* these more modest, Anglo-Indian hotels valiantly strove to convey in the most piquant contrast to their exotic surroundings a mirror image of their Victorian counterparts in Bognor Regis or Cromer. As a type, the Anglo-Indian resort hotel appeared simultaneously in Malaysia and Sri Lanka.

At Kandy, the *Queen's Hotel* would seem to be Sri Lanka's

The Governor's residence, the future
Mount Lavinia, in 1830.

earliest surviving hotel. It opened in 1849, when the beauty and relatively temperate climate of this former capital of the Vikrama kings, with its famous "Temple of the Tooth", built on the banks of a lake surrounded by hills, encouraged the British to develop their establishment there as a hot weather resort. Built in the now familiar classical-colonnade-and-verandah Anglo-Indian hotel style, with the deep eaves and tiled roofs that characterize traditional buildings in the tropical zone, the hotel occupies a prime site on the Esplanade overlooking the lake. An Edwardian refronting in a more formal French second Empire derived style, with square-domed towers, was only partially carried out and the interiors retain all their spacious Victorian-Edwardian charm complete with pilastered dining-room, billiard-room and verandah-bar.

In the second half of the 19th century Colombo became known as the "Charing Cross of the East", the pivotal port of call for liners to all points further north or east, in the Indian Ocean or the South China Sea.

Colombo's *Galle Face Hotel,* overlooking the old race course and the Indian Ocean, opened in 1864 in what had formerly been a neo-classical, colonnaded and porticoed bungalow built around 1810-20. A south wing with an octagonal pavilion and colonnaded verandah was added for the purposes of the hotel. However, by the mid-1890s, the expansion of tourism and the rivalry of such new hotels as the *Bristol* and the *Grand Continental* in the city centre engendered a major rebuilding. The classical idiom, with the addition of slight Italianate features, was nevertheless faithfully adhered to: colonnaded verandahs, a *porte cochère* and colonnaded loggias surmounting the flanking pavilions to exploit the ocean view. The most spectacular of the classical interiors is the great, two-storey arcaded ballroom while a monumental arcade theme articulates the corridors.

Mount Lavinia Hotel, opened in 1877, near Colombo, was another conversion of an early 19th-century building — in this instance a summer residence of the British Governor of Ceylon. It was built around 1825 to the designs of Captain Du Verner of the Engineers. Splendidly sited on an outcrop of rock above the sea, this elegant Palladian villa became a sought-after hotel in 1877 or even earlier and subsequent extensions have kept to the house's original character.

The *Bristol* and the *Grand Oriental Hotels* were built by the harbour on York Street, Colombo, in the late 1880 and 1890s. The *Bristol's* knowledgeably proportioned, two-tier Renaissance arcaded facades were doubtless an influence on the *Galle Face Hotel's* interiors, while the *Grand Oriental* also displayed Italianate features and had long screened verandah balconies.

MALAYSIA AND SINGAPORE:
THE EMPIRE OF THE SARKIES

Following the lead given by Singapore's 1839 *London Hotel* (later, the *Europe*) similar Anglo-Indian style hotels were opened in and around the older Straits Settlements base of Penang as the hinterland of the Malay peninsula was developed. The Armenian Sarkies brothers, founders of an oriental hotel empire, established themselves in Penang in the 1860s. Tigran and Martin Sarkies' first venture, the *Eastern Hotel*, opened in Georgetown, Penang, in 1884. A year later the *Oriental Hotel* was established close by, with the help of the third Sarkies brother, Aviet. Both were adaptations of early 19th-century porticoed Anglo-Indian bungalows. They thrived and by 1892, when Tigran was already building up the *Raffles* in Singapore, the youngest brother Arshak was called in to continue the two establishments now known as the *Eastern and Oriental Hotel.* The renowned *E&O* equipped with 100 bedrooms had extended elegant colonial facades along the spectacular sweep of its seafront lawn. In 1922, Arshak built the "Victory Annexe" crowned by oriental

Pavilions of the *Crag Hotel,* Penang, c. 1891.

domes, which was linked the next year to the main range by an opulent ballroom, giving the hotel an unprecedented 280-metre long seafront. In 1927, Arshak embarked on an over-ambitious remodelling of the *E&O*, which bankrupted him. He left behind the new entrance pavilion built in a monumental deco-classical style.

In its heyday, 1884-1927, the Sarkies' Oriental Hotel Empire at various times encompassed the *Crag*, a picturesque grouping of 1880s bungalows on top of Penang Hill, the *Raffles Grosvenor* and *Sea View* hotels, Penang; the *Strand* in Rangoon; and Singapore's *Adelphi* as well as hotel interests in Indonesia. But the jewel in the Sarkies' crown was of course the great Singapore *Raffles*. As with

Publicity postcard for the *Europe Hotel*, Singapore.

the rival *Europe Hotel* nearby, the hotel's genesis was a house of the type designed by Coleman for Singapore's founder, Sir Stamford Raffles, in their development of the town in the 1820s. Acquired and adapted by the Sarkies brothers in 1887, the house on Beach Road became the new *Raffles Hotel*. It had 40 bedrooms, each with its own bathroom (a rarity at this date), was completely fitted out with European furniture and had a 4-table billiard room — as essential a status symbol for an oriental hotel as a swimming pool is today. By 1890, Tigran Sarkies had added two more verandah-galleried wings, flanking what was to become the famous Palm Court.

The imperial apotheosis of *Raffles* was confirmed following the Sarkies' substantial and luxurious rebuilding of the hotel in 1897, when the elevations assumed their present Franco-Italianate Renaissance garb to designs by R.A.J. Bidwell. The original entrance, between the splayed corner pavilions, led through the lobby (now the Long Bar) into the "largest dining room in the East". Indeed, in decoration and scale, this long gallery with its grand staircase at the far end, recalled nothing so much as the dining halls of contemporary P&O liners. The *Raffles* in 1897, which consisted of one-hundred suites of apartments, had the first electric lighting in Singapore, its own

dynamos supplying 800 bulbs, 5 arc lamps over the entrance, and electric fans in the principal rooms; in the bedrooms, however, the *punkah wallah* still did his duty. It was at the *Raffles'* Long Bar, that the "Singapore Gin Sling" was invented in 1915. Famed from Cairo to Bombay, from California to Hong Kong, the *Raffles* remains a favoured haunt of orient-enamoured travellers and authors. The parting accolade must remain with Somerset Maugham: "There are many *Ritzs, Excelsiors, Mandarins* ... but there is only one *Raffles* ... . It stands for all the fables of the exotic East."

The *Europe Hotel* was rebuilt in 1904 on an Edwardian-palace scale with a giant colonnade inspired by Paris' Place de la Concorde as well as a grand galleried dining room. It succeeded in maintaining its reputation as the "peninsula's premier hotel" for some years before it closed in 1934, and later demolished in 1936.

Goodwood Park Hotel, built as the Teutonia Club in 1906 and converted to a hotel in 1926, continues to mount a respectable challenge to the *Raffles*. Its presence is signalled with considerable bravura by its turreted corner entrance pavilion exotically blending baroque forms, enriched with white mouldings on a grey-blue ground in the manner of Wedgwood Jasparware.

INDONESIA:

THE AMSTERDAM SCHOOL

It was in the 1930s that the hotel sector in Dutch Indonesia experienced a real growth, spurred by the expansion of oriental business and tourism. A spate of new hotel development took place, in line with Dutch government policy. Until then, and with rare exceptions, the hotels of Bali, Java and Sumatra had been relatively modest. But, with the rising popularity of the oriental cruise and the

Façade of *the Manila Hotel*, Manila.

Recently
Visited
by
Their Majesties
The King and Queen
of Siam
Their Royal Highnesses
The Crown Prince
and Princess
of Belgium
His Highness
The Susuhunan
of Solo
His Excellency
The Gouverneur
General
of Indo-China
Her Grace
Catherine; Duchess
of Westminster

The renowned „Rijsttafel" Ceremony at the

GRAND HOTEL HOMANN
BANDOENG
President: Fr. J. A. VAN ES

Façade and advertising for the *Grand Hotel Homann,* Bandoeng, c. 1930.

high reputation of the Dutch national KPM liners and, in 1931, the introduction of the Imperial Airways flying-boat service to the Far East, modern tourist accommodation was called for, on a large scale.

To meet this need, existing hotel companies sponsored by the Dutch colonial government initiated a programme of works, which included the modernization and enlargement of existing hotels and the building of new ones — ranging from residential country clubs to full-blown Grand Hotels in the larger urban centres. Dutch architects were employed for this work and the results were as architecturally enlightened as they were varied, all facets of architectural thought then current in Holland being reflected in the buildings so produced. Whether it was the thoroughgoing Dudok-influenced modernism of the *Grand Hotel Savoy-Homann* in Bandoeng, the more urban *Grand Hotel Preanger* in the same Javanese city — so strongly reminiscent of H.P. Berlage's contemporary

Gemeente Museum in The Hague, or the *Hotel Juliana* at Lahat, South Sumatra, so fittingly treated in a manner closely akin to the rural buildings produced in Holland by members of the Amsterdam School, these Indonesian hotels were entirely free of the commercialized, debased stylistic expedients so widely adopted in the design of Grand Hotels elsewhere in the Orient. If Frank Lloyd Wright's now demolished *Imperial Hotel*, Tokyo is the only Grand Hotel in the Far East to have received international architectural acclaim to date, the Dutch-influenced hotels of Indonesia richly deserve their place in the architectural-historical limelight.

THE PHILIPPINES:

THE AMERICAN INFLUENCE

As with the other colonial powers, the United States was to adapt the Grand Hotels to its own tastes and needs. It became a colonial power in the South China Sea by its acquisition of former Spanish territories, including the Philippines, as a consequence of its success in the Spanish-American war of 1898. The *Manila Hotel* was conceived as a monument to Americanism in the Philippines. Splendidly sited overlooking Manila harbour, embowered in lush tropical gardens, the 149-bedroom *Manila Hotel* was built from 1908 to 1912, to designs by the Paris-Beaux-Arts trained architect William Parsons, who was appointed directly by the first civilian governor of the Philippines, Judge William Howard Taft. Although planned in the axial Beaux-Arts manner, the general treatment and detailing of the building would seem, ironically, to have been inspired by the simple Spanish haciendas and mission buildings of Mexico and California. The interiors, however, were fitted out to American standards and were decorated in a mix of "dixhuitième" and Early Renaissance styles, executed to the very highest standards of workmanship. The *Manila* was, and remains, one of the most prestigious hotels of the Orient.

HONG KONG:

PENINSULA HOTEL

The reputation of the *Manila Hotel* may well have been one of the major reasons for the building in Hong Kong of a new Grand Hotel of international standing. Plans for the *Peninsula Hotel* to be built in the heart of Hong Kong's commercial centre in Kowloon, were drawn up immediately after the First World War. Work started on the site in 1922, for a scheduled opening in 1924. But progress was delayed by civil war in China and the doors of the *Peninsula Hotel* did not open until 1928. Built for the long-established Hong Kong Hotel Company, the *Peninsu-*

la was designed by Palmer and Turner who, at this period were also working on the *Cathay Hotel* in Shanghai. Aimed at a cosmopolitan clientèle drawn predominantly from the Americas, the hotel was truly monumental in the American sense, with a cultural whiff of the Venetian palazzo about its crowning. Internally, its most spectacular feature was the gigantic marble-floored lobby, grandiloquently decked out with white and gold in a classically derived mannerist idiom, and claimed to be "the crossroads of East and West". The *Peninsula* has been little changed and remains Hong Kong's premier hotel.

INDOCHINA

A PARISIAN SETTING

French Indochina had between 1867-87 become, after North Africa, the second centre of the "Empire Français". Its capital, Saigon was developed as a city along classic French lines. Well served by the Messageries Maritimes liners, Saigon became a fashionable port of call on the oriental circuit. The *Continental Palace* and the *Grand Hôtel de la Rotonde* were typical French colonial hotels of the 1870s and 80s, their shaded terrace-cafés providing a

Mr Palmer, founder of the well-known architectural firm "Palmer and Turner" which designed a number of grand hotels in Asia.

Parisian ambience and were a focal point of colonial society. Their dignified, rational elevations were articulated by giant orders of pilasters. The *Rotonde* was distinguished by its elegant iron-and-glass café-verandah and entrance canopy. Similar establishments were to be found in Haiphong and other main towns, while more modest bungalow hotels (claiming to be "grand" or even "palaces") were built in coast and hill resorts. By the 1920s, genuinely Grand Hotels, manifesting the span of contemporary French styles from Beaux Arts Deco to the regional, were being developed to meet the expanding oriental cruise market and to provide accommodation near such historical temple sites as the Angkor Wat.

Guests of the *Grand Hôtel de Pékin* seeking refuge in a pavilion of the British legation during the "Boxer Rebellion", Peking, 1900.

CHINA:

CATHAY HOTEL AND GRAND HOTEL DE PEKIN

China's military and political weakness in the 19th century inevitably tempted foreign aggression and commercial exploitation. After the cession of Hong Kong to Britain in 1842, China was increasingly subject to inroads from the colonial powers, initially Britain and France, followed by Russia and at the end of the century the United States and the new expansionist power of Emperor Meiji's Japan. China's principal harbours were opened up to foreign trade, where Western enclaves were established. In 1858, the Chinese "violation" of the Treaty of Tientsin resulted in the Franco-British occupation of Peking and the creation there of the European embassy quarter.

Shanghai became the main port of arrival. It developed as a Western-style city with a magnificent urban elevation extending along the Bund — the waterfront where the principal buildings and hotels were located. An Italianate "palazzo" style was favoured in the 1870s and long

The *Oriental Hotel,* Kobe, c. 1920.

The *Yamada Hotel,* Yamada, c. 1930.

remained popular, so that when the *Central Hotel* (on the Bund, by the main landing stage) was rebuilt on a grand scale in 1906 as the *Palace Hotel*, its elevations were still decked out with Italianate motifs, while the Edwardian classical interiors followed the example set by the *Raffles* in Singapore. Shanghai's international heyday as the business and social mecca of the Orient came in the late 1920s and '30s, following the establishment of Chiang Kai-shek's Nationalist government. This period coincided with the Jazz Age and the development of Shanghai's skyscraper studded skyline along the pattern of Manhattan. The *Palace Hotel* was dwarfed by the new *Cathay Hotel*, a gigantic stripped-down classical multistorey pile crowned by a copper-clad pyramid that remains a prominent landmark on the Bund. Built between 1926 to 1931, the Cathay was designed by the Hong Kong and Shanghai-based architectural practice of Palmer and Turner, who were responsible for most of the major high-rise buildings of the period in Shanghai as well as the famous *Peninsula*

Hotel in Hong Kong, where they remain a well-known practice there. Cosmopolitan Shanghai society revolved around the *Cathay's* world-famous roof-top restaurant and dance-floor, shimmying to the latest sound of a Chicago Big Band throughout the '30s. Following the 1949 Communist take over, the *Cathay Hotel* — with its splendid Art Deco period interiors — was merged with its neighbour, the *Palace Hotel.* The combined facilities are now known as the *Peace Hotel.*

The first major hotel catering to Westerners to be built in Beijing was the *Grand Hôtel de Pékin*, which opened in the 1890s, in the Embassy quarter, near Tien-an-men Square and next to the Imperial Palace. Originally undistinguished in appearance, the *Grand Hôtel de Pékin* was substantially remodelled and enlarged from the early 1920s onwards, in the then prevalent simplified classicism of the Anglo-American Beaux-Arts style, with interiors to match. As it was completed in the 1950s under the Communist regime, a Chinese interpretation of Soviet

Socialist classicism was externally blended with the 1920s building, the more traditional Chinese touches being applied to the grand interiors.

The similarly named but completely separate *Hôtel de Pékin*, opened in 1903, was the furthest flung outpost of the Compagnie Internationale des Wagons-Lits' chain. Of simple classical design, its quadrangular layout centred on that ubiquitous feature, the Palm Court. This device was by then so firmly associated with the East as to be taken up in European hotels of the period as an instant evocation of the Orient. Although the *Hôtel de Pékin* building still survives, it is no longer used as an hotel.

JAPAN:

A FUSION OF EAST AND WEST

In 1854, Commodore Perry's naval threat to Tokyo compelled Japan to grant trade concessions and privileges to the United States. Similar agreements followed with the European powers and, for the first time in over two centuries, Japan and its ports opened up to the world. The first modest European hotels, of a conventional colonnaded verandah type, appeared in the late 1860s and '70s, on the waterfronts of such treaty ports as Kobe and Yokohama as they had in China. This accessibility to what had been a closed country soon attracted orientalist tourists and, in return, saw the flowering of *Japonaiserie* taste in the West. Ensuing hotel development however, was not restricted to tightly-defined European enclaves, as was the case in China in 1868. European advisors were called in and, in barely three decades, Japan emerged from feudal isolation to become an industrial and colonizing power.

The first manifestation of this policy, so far as hotel building was concerned, was fundamentally Western in concept. By the Emperor Meiji's death in 1912, Tokyo Station incorporated a grand terminus hotel with domes, turrets and baroque trimmings that would have been equally at home in Central Europe or the States. Kyoto, Kobe and the new industrial centre of Osaka had all acquired large hotel establishments in the European classical revival styles, most notably the *Oriental Hotel* at Kobe. This phenomenon was equally evident in Japan's newly acquired colonies. In Dairen, seized from China in 1894, the *Yamato Hotel* was built in 1905, with "Dixhuitième" interiors and a grand Beaux-Arts facade of the kind made internationally fashionable by the 1900 Paris Exhibition.

Very soon, however, the Japanese began to tailor their own traditional building forms to provide accommodation for Western and other tourists. An early instance of this

The *Yamato Hotel,* Dalian, c. 1920.

vernacular transposition was the *Fujiya Hotel* at Miyanoshita, Hakone (where there are hot springs and fine views of Mount Fuji). It opened in 1878 to cater specifically to European tourists and the original building was burnt down six years later. Early photographs show a European colonial arrangement of verandahs with turned balusters applied to a multistorey reinterpretation of traditional Japanese timber-frame construction, with large overhanging eaves and tiled roofs. Rebuilt in 1884 and restored after the 1923 earthquake, the hotel took on a more Westernized aspect. It was treated as a group of three bay-fronted Victorian-Edwardian style villas. Nonetheless, the pavilion massing, roof lines and "eyebrow" porch details are all in the Japanese tradition. By 1936, Japanese and Western idioms were further combined in the new "Flower Palace Wing" of the *Fujiya*, where Japanese motifs are applied to an overall form of Western origin.

It was, however, the *Nara Hotel*, designed by Kingo Tatsumi and Yasu Katao, which opened in Nara city in 1909 that provided the most successful fusion of the traditional Japanese timber-framed Imperial palace-type with the European Grand Hotel. Here, an extended pavilion layout with verandahs was arranged around a two-storey lobby off which a grand staircase led to Western-style suites of guest rooms on the upper floors. Dining room, lounge, restaurant and other public rooms occupied the ground floors. This basically European layout was overlaid with a magnificent display of traditional motifs executed in cypress-woods of the finest quality and the furniture and fittings were executed in the latest European styles. The *Nara Hotel* remains one of the most prestigious hotels in Japan and survives virtually unchanged.

The culmination of cross-cultural aspirations was the *Imperial Hotel*, Tokyo, designed for the Great Japan Hotel Company by Frank Lloyd Wright in 1916. As is evident from his earlier work in the United States, Wright had long been interested in Japanese art and architecture. The apogee of his achievement in that direction is the *Imperial Hotel*, for there he succeeded not only in reinterpreting Japanese idioms in what might be described as an away match, but did so by using construction techniques far better adapted to Japanese conditions than were those traditionally used there. The *Imperial* was inaugurated in 1923, when it was one of the very few buildings to survive the major earthquake that devastated Japan. Sadly, the *Imperial* no longer stands in Tokyo; it was demolished in 1967 to make place for a modern hotel.

GRAND HOTELS
AND PALACES

The development of the oriental hotel, from its origins as a classically derived bungalow adapted to local climatic conditions to its ultimate full-blown, commercialized supra-palatial form, combined two distinct functions: firstly, it served as a local social centre and secondly, as a place for a passing population of businessmen and tourists. Originally a comfortable setting where the white man could indulge his sense of superiority while temporarily escaping the rigours of colonial administration or business dealings, these hotels provided a refuge where visitors could be sure of finding all the necessities of European life while providing them with a safe vantage point from which to sample the exoticism of the East.

As the white man's supremacy in the Grand Hotels of the Orient was gradually eroded in the post-war period, when the upper echelons of the newly independent national states took a socially equal — and often superior — place among the Western clientèle, the evolution of the Grand Hotels was to take a new twist, both architecturally and socially.

One of the best examples exemplifying this new trend is the recent renovation of the magnificent Indian palaces, built by Indian princes in the period between Queen Victoria's coronation as Empress of India in 1877 and Indian Independence in 1947. These princes, who had prospered under the Raj, had built a great many luxurious palaces, often incorporating lavish and completely separate establishments for their "untouchable" European guests.

In 1970, these princes were suddenly deprived of their more than generous state pensions. As their now redundant princely palaces offered a far more exotic and enticing bait for well-off Western tourists than did any of the stereotyped modern international hotel, the newly insolvent Indian princes found themselves with the potential for an instant alternative form of income. Some sold out lock, stock, and barrel, while others were able to retain their own palatial accommodation through agreements with Indian hotel chains, which took over and converted to luxury hotel use premises originally designed for guests — often in the form of an independent palace complete with its own service arrangements.

The cosmopolitan clientèle attracted to this new form of oriental Grand Hotel naturally includes many Westerners, who no longer go to India as a self-appointed "superior" colonizing race, but briefly to indulge in truly oriental splendour.

Baggage label, 1930s.

RENDEZVOUS

AT THE SHEPHEARD'S

by Joseph Fitchett

The great hotels of the Orient were a unique setting for a fascinating cast of characters, aristocrats and tycoons, swindlers and whores. The hotels were oases, where Western travellers and expatriates were on their own ground; mirages of familiarity amid the populous, indifferent and troubling societies of Arabs and Persians, Indians and Turks, Chinese and Japanese. These grand establishments — often as famous as the palaces or monuments in a city — were the scenes of glamorous triumphs and savage dramas during the century when the West tried to hustle the East.

The allure of these hotels in the Middle East and North Africa was still strong in the post-war years, right up to the oil-price boom and social convulsions of the 1970s. The new wealth — described by some as "the curse of so little land and so much oil" — irrevocably transformed the face of the region, for better in prosperity and for worse in stability. Progress swept away most of the old landmarks, many of them violently. Progress also brought hotels with international-style superficial comforts. The romance of grand establishments is hard to recapture, but living and working there for nearly a decade gave me vivid glimpses of the charms of the old order before these changes.

How quickly and totally such a way of life will recede from memory. This was borne in on me as I moved back to the West and began to travel among the capitals of Europe and North America, inevitably living and often working in hotels. In the Middle East, I had haunted the hotels' lobbies and dining rooms, bars and swimming-pools. Now I found myself retreating to my room, shunning the public rooms where the suburban conversations could have been heard on a crossed phone-line, a sad come-down from the suggestive, whispered confidences of politicians and spies, adventuresses and writers which made for exciting eavesdropping in the great establishments of Arab capitals. My

sense of disappointment crystallized for me in a conversation with Yusef Karsh, the Armenian-born portrait photographer. One of his strongest memories, he said, was the intensity of his wartime nights in London's *Savoy Hotel*, where British leaders and entertainers regularly gathered during the Nazi blitz to drink and talk after hours, occasionally venturing drunkenly onto the hotel's roof to shout obscenities at the invisible enemy overhead. When he described that scene I thought of other great traditions at other hotels — the New York wits at the Round Table in the *Algonquin*, Marcel Proust's dinner parties at the *Ritz* in Paris, Hemingway making love in a Barcelona hotel room to the sound of incoming rounds of fire during the Spanish civil war. Thinking back on the heyday of the great hotels of the West, now lost forever except in resorts, I realized that my fascination with the intense life of the Orient's great hotels was partly fed by nostalgia for a period I never knew, an era of intense urbanity in Western living. Like the half-life of a nuclear detonation, the great colonial hotels echoed a romantic moment in Western history, the moment when the centre of social life moved out of the palaces and cloisters, the clubs and mansions of traditional society and flourished in the restaurants and hotels open to all comers.

Hotels had a special place in the closed societies of the Moslem world and the Orient. As the conservative Ottoman Empire crumbled a hundred years ago and Westerners penetrated the Middle East and North Africa in swelling numbers, hotels were a means of keeping the foreigners and the locals out of each other's hair. On grand occasions, they were also the only suitable accommodation for large groups of prominent people, enabling local leaders to play host on their own soil without imposing their own rules on food and women's movements. With their quasi-extraterritorial status, they were cocoons for tourists, venues for meetings of state, military headquarters in wartime, swank annexes for local society offering liquor, dancing, gambling and even a Hollywoodian backdrop for local weddings — not to mention a window on European living.

The *Nile Hilton*, in Cairo, for example, was just such a landmark. The place to run into both the people you know and the officials with whom you could never get an appointment, it also had a lush pool in sweltering Cairo, a coffee-shop with the first waitresses in Egypt, specially angled corridors for security surveillance and bedroom views of the Nile. In postwar times, it was the nearest thing to the old hotels.

The Grand Hotels had their heyday after the First World War. Most, even those built as late as the 1930s, were solid, spacious, Edwardian establishments, with room (and rooms) for the stately occasions and scampish hi-jinks of

The *Cecil Hotel,* Cairo, 1970s.

expatriate life. Equally important and romantic were a handful of small, inn-like hotels situated in ancient localities or at strategic crossroads: every traveller was forced by circumstances to spend time in these outposts, which acquired their own legendary auras. For example, in Palmyra, the ancient city in central Syria, travellers like Agatha Christie and her archaeologist husband all stayed at the *Zenobia*, the inn in the ruins run by the Baroness d'Andurin, a Frenchwoman in search of the wilder shores of love. In cities, too, hotels were bridgeheads into the East. As readers of Lawrence Durrell's *Alexandria Quartet* will recall, the heroine Justine, a sensual local woman, first encounters Darby, the English writer, in the *Cecil Hotel* amid dusty potted palms in the decayed hotel's gaunt vestibule. In the old Middle East, whenever East met West, it usually happened in a hotel.

KHAN TO HILTONS

These encounters were not always civilized. The glamorous hotels' high profiles often appeared as arrogance and defiance to local people, and many of them were destroyed in recent years. Their violent end was a vent to the hostility often felt about them, a hostility which was much repressed in earlier days. Prudent hotel managers were always careful to keep guests who were eating or drinking out of view of the streets. Especially during Ramadan, the Moslem month of dawn-to-dusk fasting, when sweating, exasperated workers could be driven to a righteous frenzy by the sight of foreigners sipping alcohol or smoking in defiance of local divine law. But tact of this sort was hopelessly inadequate to cope with the tensions that engulfed the Middle East in the anti-colonial ferment after the Second World War. As a symptom of that mood I remember seeing a flyblown photograph in an Egyptian museum at El-Alamein in the 1960s that showed pale women in wide hats at teatime on the elegant terrace of the old *Shepheard's* in Cairo, the most famous hotel in the Middle East. The typewritten caption read: "English spy-ladies in our land." That *Shepheard's* was burned to the ground by Egyptian mobs during the riots preceding the overthrow of the monarchy in 1952. In 1956, in the revolution in Iraq, foreigners were forcibly pulled from the main hotels in Baghdad to be dragged to death in the streets. One of the bloodiest terrorist acts of its time was the Zionists' bombing of Jerusalem's *King David Hotel*, which was one of the most prominent British civilian and military establishments in mandate Palestine. And equally heavy in both bloodshed and symbolism was the "war of hotels" in Beirut during the civil war in Lebanon when both sides, the Palestinians from the refugee camps and the Lebanese Christian village boys, poured their fury on the opulent tourist palaces, seizing them for strategic reasons and then despoiling and desecrating them with the vengeful spite reminiscent of frustrated burglars. It was a sordid, tragi-comic apocalypse for a mirage of Western glamour that had taken shape gradually over the better part of a century.

Travellers to the Middle East, prior to the mid-19th century, either packed their meagre needs with them in a humble bedroll or camped in aristocratic style. The Grand Hotel only emerged in response to the colonial influx of Westerners in the region, accompanied by tourists.

For earlier travellers — known as "Orientalists" because they were exploring the "Near East" of the Orient — accommodation consisted either of a spare room in a local potentate's palace or a cell in the fort-like *khans* or caravanserais built along caravan routes as early as the 13th century.

In traditional Arab lifestyle, hotels had no place in the local scheme of things. Hospitality was a sacred obligation, a social duty — to sell it would make a Bedouin blush — and any self-respecting traveller took an invitation to stay with relatives, friends or local notables for granted. But as commerce developed and spread, thanks to the public order established by the Moslem conquests, it became an impossible task for tribes and townsmen along the great trade routes to accommodate or even protect the growing caravans. So the first *khans* appeared — fortified single-storey buildings, enclosing a well and a central courtyard used for animals, baggage and wagons. Around the open courtyard were vaulted storerooms for goods and fodder. Built a day's journey apart, a distance of 20 to 25 miles, along the main routes, the roadside *khans* offered safe, dependable lodging to travellers, pilgrims, merchants, postal conveys — to anyone except soldiers on the march. In remote *khans,* the only accommodation was a four-foot-deep inner ledge in the courtyard wall; small hearths were spaced at intervals along it where travellers made mini-camps, cooking over a wood fire and sleeping wrapped in a saddle-blanket, with the saddle for a pillow and camels tethered at their feet. In the heat, when caravans moved at night, travellers gathered on the *khan's* flat roof in the early evening to eat and talk before the convoy moved off. The cities developed larger, multi-storeyed *khans*, some architecturally quite sophisticated. The most splendid might contain a mosque, together with a livery stable and blacksmith, plus a coffee house. The *khans* themselves were never converted into hotels. (Most surviving ones are either garages, a few were among the region's first movie theatres.) But they foreshadowed the great hotels in revealing ways. They were self-contained worlds, where travellers could be isolated from the local community of the faithful, just as hotels have continued to do in recent decades. And the form has survived in many modern establishments, from the region's oldest hotel, the *Bassoul* in Beirut, to the most ambitious recent hotel, the *Shah Abbas* in Ispahan which, before the Khomeini revolution in Iran tried to recapture the splendour and style of Persia's past. Like *khans*, they retained the feature of locating bedrooms around a courtyard, now enclosed to become a lobby, so that the traveller, perhaps feeling isolated and lonely, had only to open the door to find conviviality in the hotel's main public space.

Of course, the old arrangements in *khans* (or in their later urban equivalents, the dormitory-like *funduks*) would not do for Westerners who were not Orientalists and wanted familiar comforts. They wanted more privacy, Western-style toilets, mosquito-netting over their beds, food resembling the kind they were used to and, perhaps most important of all, a comfortable haven where the reassuring sound of European voices helped to ward off the shock of confronting a foreign culture. Even today, staying in modern hotels in the Middle-East, I constantly see their lobbies, restaurants and shopping arcades packed with local expatriates who drop in for an hour or two, hoping to enjoy the illusion of being home. This mood of relief and feeling of security from regaining familiar surroundings — safe from the alien streets — is strongly caught in movies such as Hitchcock's scenes in Morocco in *The Man Who Knew Too Much* and even in Rick's American Cafe in *Casablanca*.

FLAUBERT IN EGYPT

Early travellers revelled in the exotic. Gustave Flaubert, then 29, travelled with the French man of letters (and early travel photographer) Maxime du Camp through Egypt and Lebanon and Turkey in 1850. The trip infused Flaubert's mind with images that he eventually used to great effect in his historical novel, *Salammbô*. They embraced the East in all its sensuality. When they went up the Nile to visit the ancient temples at Luxor, du Camp discovered "an English hotel near the ruins, offering 'furnished apartment and mock turtle, accompanied by bottles of pale ale', where I drank clean water and ate hard-boiled eggs without suffering any after-effects: an admirable advance of civilization or perhaps of exploitation which I admire, but which I don't regret not having encountered any sooner on this trip." Despite their disdain for superficial imitations of European lifestyles and enthusiasm for the Orient's mysteries, hotels punctuate their trip. Flaubert notes that it was "in a little street right behind the *Hôtel d'Orient*" where the two men were staying — and which also served as the consulate of Tuscany — that he finally (and proudly) managed to sample a belly dancer's ultimate favours.

Publicity card, 1920s.

Flaubert scathingly observed hotels' pathetic attempts to look modern in their decoration. Staying in Cairo's *Hôtel du Nil*, he recorded that the first-floor hallway was decorated with lithographs by the popular contemporary illustrator Gavarni: they were only pages torn out of the weekly satiric Paris magazine, *Charivari* — the "quintessence of Parisianism, which is what civilization sends here." But Flaubert's attention was also often turned to France: du Camp records the novelist staring at the second cataract, halfway up the Nile, and suddenly shouting, "I've got it! Eureka! Eureka! I'll call her Emma Bovary." The owner of the *Hôtel du Nil*, where they had stayed in Cairo, was "Bouvaret".

As westernization started to invade Egypt, however, the adventurous few, who wanted a "voyage in the Orient", had to move farther afield, mainly to Arabia. In Egypt, new hordes of businessmen and tourists created a market for European-style hotels.

LEGENDARY *SHEPHEARD'S*

This change in travel pattern between Europe and Asia occurred with the opening of the Suez Canal in 1869. The British began travelling to India via Egypt and the Red Sea (rather than around the Cape). The establishment that eventually became the most celebrated hostelry outside Europe was founded in Egypt in 1841 when Samuel Shepheard, a Victorian businessman who had been involved in managing relay inns on the overland route from Cairo to the Red Sea, set up a Cairo boarding house that eventually became *Shepheard's Hotel*. For a century, it was an institution — the hub of life in the capital for expatriates and for Westernized Egyptians. Today, the Nileside *Shepheard's*, built in the garish concrete and

Entrance of the *Shepheard's,* Cairo, photo by Bonfils,
end of the last century.

lumpy Art Deco that was in favour in the 1950s in Egypt, conveys little hint of the grandeur and liveliness that made *Shepheard's* a world rendezvous for decades. Nonetheless, on my last visit, there was still something in the dignified service (and in the extraordinary services of a hotel masseuse in the basement) that suggested *Shepheard's* has not entirely forgotten its institutional memories of lofty grandeur lifting it above its surroundings and local ways. *Shepheard's* needed all its morale to cope with the tensions that accompanied its extraordinary success and its equally extraordinary crises. With growth, it has changed site thrice and has been rebuilt four times, once after it was razed by fire on "Black Saturday" in 1952 when Egyptian mobs raged through the Cairo streets protesting against British influence. The plaque you see in the entrance hall conveys the saga in outline:"SHEPHEARD'S HOTEL, founded in 1841 by Mr Samuel Shepheard of Preston Capes as the New Shepheard's Hotel, afterwards Shepheard's

British Hotel on the site once occupied by Napoleon's Headquarters."

The original *Shepheard's* was set up in a former harem in Ezbekiyah, a Cairo neighbourhood renowned for its greenery. The low lying area had once been swamp, then drained to make room for a pleasant square alive with coffee shops and surrounded by leafy paths. Travellers crowded the cafes, listening to open-air concerts. In conformity with general practice throughout the Ottoman Empire, non-Egyptians were to some extent segregated from the local Moslems, and so foreign communities and consulates in Cairo were confined to the Ezbekiyah district. The gates leading to it were locked each night, and the government declined to take any responsibility for the safety of foreigners who were left outside the walled enclave. *Shepheard's* itself was a plain building, with balconies on the top storey which were decorated with the wooden grilles to facilitate the flow of air and provide privacy for the occupants. Its most celebrated feature was a broad terrace that gave guests an uninterrupted and slightly elevated view of the street life of the East.

In a hard-to-find history of *Shepheard's Hotel,* Nina Nelson writes: "Every nationality, rich and poor, strolled in the square [in front of the hotel]. It was not unusual to see a Frankish lady in the latest Paris hat making way for an urchin on donkeyback or a pack of half wild dogs. The whole area was surrounded by a low canal with grassy banks; shepherds watered their flocks, as they had in the days of the Bible, while they watched, wide-eyed, the passing throng: Turks garbed in bright, rich silks, glossy negroes in long white robes and vermillion turbans, quick-witted Greeks, Jewish money-lenders, snake-charmers and conjurers, handsome Egyptians and fashionable tourists.

"Each morning, visitors would emerge from the cool interior of the hotel through a plain wooden door which gave straight onto the street and over which hung a great bronze lantern. Donkeys were hired from the donkey boys who hung round the entrance [like competitive, multi-lingual taxi-drivers who hang around the *Nile Hilton* today]. After much bargaining and gesticulating, a price would be arranged and the patient beasts would be mounted by ladies in full, ample skirts and hats with flowing ostrich plumes escorted by gentlemen in swallow-tailed coats and peg-top trousers, who would then ride off unconcernedly through the city's tortuous lanes, pursued by the tireless donkey boys, perhaps to watch bargaining in the slave market, visit a mosque and shop in the bazaars, or go grotting off to the Pyramids."

Once ensconced in *Shepheard's,* it was easy to forget that forbidding and even murderous deserts were only a few miles away. The hotel was a welcome haven for travellers, who disembarked at the Mediterranean port of Alexandria and then had to travel to Cairo by canal ferry. Travellers coming West found *Shepheard's* a paradise after coaches brought them overland to Cairo from Suez, where they

Shepheard's, Cairo, c. 1910.

39

Gardens of the *Gezira Palace*.

had disembarked after travelling through the inferno of the Red Sea. A letter-writer who travelled that dusty road recorded: "Those who may have travelled across the Isthmus in summer will recall with gratitude their plunge into the big stone baths in the lower regions of *Shepheard's Hotel*." Guests revelled in the waving trees of the hotel's big garden, which included, among the date palms and acacias, a sycamore bearing a plague: "Général Kléber". The tree had hidden the assassin who stabbed Kléber to death while the French commander of Napoleon's army in Egypt was strolling in the garden of his headquarters. Inside, the hotel had acquired the amenities needed to be a world complete unto itself. Shops — even a post office — were established The high-ceilinged Moorish decor became more elaborate. A hotel restaurant freed guests of the necessity of having to travel with their own cooks.

In only 20 years, Shepheard, at the early age of 40, had amassed a fortune enabling him to retire to Britain. A US Consul wrote in the hotel's golden book: "Shepheard left behind him a name that is identified with Egypt and with Cairo as closely as it would have been had its owner built a pyramid."

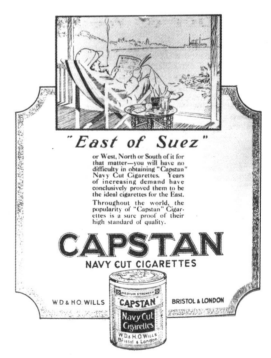

The pleasure of English cigarettes in the Orient.

THE "SEASON" IN EGYPT

The gala opening of the Suez Canal gave Egypt an occasion to construct several new hotels to join *Shepheard's* on what became Opera Square, opposite the brand-new Opera House, a wood and plaster edifice painted the same dull apricot as *Shepheard's*.

Only months before the Canal's inauguration, *Shepheard's* was partly burnt, but it was quickly rebuilt, this time in the form of a hollow square structure and, like many oriental palaces, it came with a courtyard. To accentuate the exotic decor, two small sphinxes were brought from an excavation to flank the entrance.

The opening of Ferdinand de Lesseps' Suez Canal in November was the most celebrated event of the decade in Egypt. Empress Eugénie, the wife of Napoleon III, was invited to inaugurate the opening. It was the most sumptuous season in Cairo's modern history. Eugénie stayed in the *Gezira Palace* which subsequently became a palatial hotel, the *Omar Khayyam*. The hotel (now bought over by the Marriott chain) remained intact until the 1970s, with its fountains and gardens from Eugénie's day and even her bedroom, which was a replica of her private apartments in the Tuileries Palace in Paris. Many of the most glamorous moments occurred in hotels. A sumptuous banquet was held at *Shepheard's* for Empress Eugénie. She was considered the most beautiful woman of her generation, and crowds gathered to catch a glimpse of her as she left the lavishly-decorated dining room and the hotel.

Shepheard's was the hub of Cairo's whirl of international celebrities, and among its guests none more colourful or famous in his day than the French writer Théophile Gautier. It was his first visit to Egypt and he was enchanted by *Shepheard's*. He had a large, rug-strewn room, with a view over the rose gardens and a skyline of roofs and palm trees, domes and minarets against the yellow hills. Gautier, recuperating from a broken arm he suffered on the voyage, used binoculars to watch the picturesque characters in the street from the verandah. Each evening, the hotel rang a gigantic Chinese gong to announce that dinner time was approaching. Guests retired to their rooms to change, then went to dinner, where professional groups or social cliques often occupied regular tables. Gautier liked *Shepheard's* French-style cooking and wines, the discreet service of white-gloved waiters and the formality of the meals. When the ladies retired after dinner, the men stayed on to talk over coffee, brandy and cigars.

With the Suez Canal operating, Port Said and Suez became the important trading stations, with hotels catering to businessmen. Cairo, however, also benefitted from the

View from a room of the *Mena House Hotel*.

surge in tourism fuelled by the publicity that the Canal opening received throughout the West. Egypt's dry atmosphere and winter warmth attracted the elderly and convalescent. A *Shepheard's* brochure claimed that for many ailments, air is the supreme remedy: "Let a man come as far east as Cairo and sit but for an hour in the sun of *Shepheard's Terrace* and watch the world go by, or stroll for but an hour down the tortuous Mousky [the Cairo bazaar]; let him but hear the call to prayer from a minaret, the blind beggar chant verses from the Koran; let him see a native sail take on a wondrous grace in the wind of a Nile sunset — let him see all this and more, and he will be a new man!"

Shepheard's, by 1890, had become so popular that the chronic problem of how to get a room there in season had become a nightmare. In tackling the problem, the management took drastic action, pulling down the building with its many annexes and erecting in its place a modern hotel with all the latest amenities and increased the number of bedrooms and bathrooms. The new hotel, still a rectangular building around a courtyard with fountains and palm trees, had the Italian style typical of the period. The famous terrace replaced the low balcony along the hotel's front.

The new hotel ranked as one of the world's most elaborate hotels of the day. *Shepheard's* became the first hotel in the Middle East to have electric lighting, supplied by a private generator in the garden. Another innovation was the installation of the steam laundry in the basement. The director's office was built directly over the spot where Kléber had been stabbed to death, and the sycamore tree that was his assassin's hiding place could be seen from his office window. The main ground-floor passage was hung with paintings of Egypt and etchings, lithographs and drawings of state occasions at *Shepheard's*.

Shepheard's was a national institution. For tourists, it could arrange excursions to watch dervishes ride horses over the bodies of their devout followers. For Cairenes, it was sought after for society weddings. *Shepheard's* had become synonymous in travellers' minds with Cairo — like *Raffles* in Singapore, an inseparable part of foreigners' impressions of the country.

IN THE SHADE OF THE PYRAMIDS

Competition soon grew. An English couple, Mr and Mrs Locke, who had wintered near the Pyramids for their health, were so taken with the experience that they bought the small inn and started *Mena House*. Rebuilt as a manor house with rare antique Oriental furnishings, *Mena House* offered the unique attraction of an uninterrupted view of the Pyramids. On moonlit nights, a pleasant way of viewing the Pyramids and the Sphinx was to dine at *Mena House*. The hotel orchestra was in attendance for tea and dinner. After dinner it was time for a horseback ride around the great monuments. In Cairo itself each hotel had its "night," and those who today would be called the Beautiful People rotated from hotel to hotel.

Veterans of *Shepheard's* were also involved in starting the *Continental Hotel*, whose owners then took over an Egyptian palace to start the *Savoy*. Under the management of a young Swiss, Auguste Wild, who had been manager at

Baggage label, 1930s.

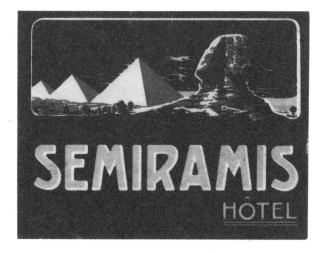

Baggage label, 1930s.

the *Baur au Lac* in Zurich, the *Savoy* became one of the most exclusive hotels in the Middle East. Wild Bey, as he was known, wrote in his memoirs, *Mixed Grill in Cairo,* that the *Savoy* regularly earned a profit of fifteen thousand pounds on a season lasting little more than four months. The newcomers thrived to a considerable extent on getting the overflow from *Shepheard's*, which was managed by another Swiss, Charles Baehler, known in his day as the "Hotel King" because of his expanding empire. Of all his hotels, he told Miss Nelson, *Shepheard's* remained his favourite (though he regarded the building of the *King David Hotel* in Jerusalem as the apex of his career).

The *Semiramis*, the first Cairo hotel on the river, was built in 1886 and located between the British Embassy and the British army base (later the site of the *Nile Hilton*). The *Semiramis* stressed luxury from the outset. Open only during the three-month winter season, the whole roof was a single suite, and there was a special mezzanine of small rooms, the *étage des courriers,* entirely for the guests' personal servants. Always an elegant hostelry, the *Semiramis* later had Cairo's first elevators (brassbound mahogany marvels still working today), its first European-style nightclub (a rooftop restaurant with an orchestra for dancing—still unsurpassed) which began when the hotel innovated by opening in summer as well as winter after the Second World War, and a renowned catering service. "The hotel with the most style in Cairo," was the local assessment.

Despite the competition *Shepheard's* remained prestigious and unique. On liners, as new travellers asked experienced fellow-passengers where they would be staying in Cairo, the answer invariably was "*Shepheard's*" ... "*Shepheard's*" ... "*Shepheard's*". An Alexandrian hotelier wrote bitterly: "The tourists of the world who come here seem to be racing against time to reach *Shepheard's* terrace."

ADVENTURERS AND EXPLORERS

In many ways *Shepheard's* was more than an ordinary successful hotel. Frequently it was the headquarters of adventurers and military men. In the 19th century, explorers of Africa used the hotel as their final staging post and jumping-off point up the Nile to Sudan and the Dark Continent. These special guests included Henry Stanley of the *New York Herald*, who found the lost missionary Dr David Livingstone, and Slatin Pasha, an explorer and administrator of the Sudan. Slatin retired in a luxury suite at *Shepheard's* after suffering terrible hardship in Sudan, but Stanley, who had mounted a major expedition from *Shepheard's*, avoided the hotel when he returned from the three-year trip in order to "avoid the lounging critics that sat in judgement upon me at *Shepheard's Hotel*." Similar views of *Shepheard's* as a corrupting influence were held by General George "Chinese" Gordon, the inspiring British colonialist who was defeated and beheaded in Khartoum by religious fanatics before a relief column could reach the city. Gordon went to his death convinced that his rescuers would never arrive in time because they were enjoying themselves at *Shepheard's*.

Shepheard's came into its own in wartime, an even more dramatic case of its growing role as an antechamber of Egypt's rulers. Lord Kitchener, an informal viceroy of Egypt for a decade at the century's end, was a retiring man who shunned official hospitality and he used *Shepheard's* extensively as a comfortable extension of his residence and office.

During the First World War, it was used as the British headquarters in the Near East (T.E. Lawrence, haunting the corridors to win support for his Arab irregulars, detested

The *Winter Palace*, Luxor, 1930s.

Shepheard's, Cairo.

the hotel as a hive of bureaucracy). Spies and profiteers hung around the hotel's Long Bar, hoping to overhear tidbits of information or strike up lucrative friendships that could be cemented in the dining room.

Tradition has it that after British forces evacuated the Dardenelles, there were over 200 generals staying at *Shepheard's*, each demanding a private bathroom when the hotel had only 270 private bathrooms for its 550 rooms.

It served also as the unofficial Allied theatre headquarters in the Second World War, and Rommel, the Germans' "Desert Fox", allegedly had wired *Shepheard's*, booking a room for himself after the victory he over-confidently anticipated against the British in North Africa. The British held at El-Alamein and kept *Shepheard's*, but could not fend off social changes. Ladies were allowed for the first time to enter the Long Bar at the back of the hotel presided over by *Shepheard's* Italian bartender, Gasperini, who was usually ready to lend good customers a few pounds. Service women were allowed to attend dances in their uniforms. The hotel teemed with correspondents. Many of them who first knew the hotel in the war years happened to be staying there on the Saturday in 1952 when the anti-British mobs turned it into an inferno.

WINTER PALACES

The attractions of the Upper Nile steadily lured tourists to venture beyond Cairo. In 1880, the Egyptian government gave Thomas Cook & Son a monopoly on passenger steamers on the Nile, and by 1890 they had 15 cruise boats operating as floating hotels. In 1887, Cook's opened a hotel at Luxor — the first Cook's hotel anywhere. Cook's in Egypt was grander and more luxurious than Cook's in

Europe, offering tourism to aristocrats and colonels (a little like the Roman tourists in ancient Egypt, many of whom were centurions on leave or visiting the sites of their old campaigns after retirement). As travellers went up the Nile from Cairo to visit the ruins of ancient Egypt, their route was studded with a chain of these winter palaces. They were a match in elegance to the steamers that carried a flow of celebrities south on the Nile to view the pharaonic splendours at Abu Simbel.

The *Winter Palace* at Luxor, with its slowly revolving ceiling fans, restored the stamina of tourists so they could visit the temple of Karnak. It commands a view across the Nile to the cliffs of the Royal Necropolis of Thebes, containing the tomb of Tutankhamen, King Tut, the discovery of which in 1922 made headlines because of the then current enthusiasm for Egyptology. Egypt had become an ideal open-air museum where it never rained. The winter palaces catered to this passion with decors and facilities for pseudo-scholarly lectures to amateurs about the lore of pharaonic dynasties. They were literally palatial. The *Winter Palace* at Luxor, for example, is a huge bright pink sandstone structure — kitsch to most people today, imposing in its day — with parquet floors, mahogany chairs and a general air of sumptuous gloom.

The finest (and still the best preserved of all the region's vintage hotels) is the *Old Cataract* at Aswan, the once-tranquil village near the great cataracts that disappeared with the construction of the Aswan High Dam. Today the *Old Cataract* evokes the splendours of past travel: its bathrooms alone are bigger than the bedrooms in many modern hotels, oriental rugs carpet the floors, the verandah steps lead down to the riverbank where *feluccas*, with their triangular sails, can be hired for picnicking on any of the small green islands dotting the great river — including one planted with the Victorian cuttings of Lord Kitchener. Indoors, the *Old Cataract* seems preserved in amber: the glass-fronted bookcases lining the library walls are packed with first editions, still dusted as regularly as they were in the days when guests spent weeks basking in the winter warmth.

NORTH AFRICA
AN EXOTIC "RIVIERA"

The same grandeur once prevailed in an equally celebrated hotel in Morocco — the *Mamounia* (now hideously disfigured by an elaborate modernization

Façade of the *Mamounia,* Marrakech, 1930s.

Dining room of the *Hôtel Saint-George,* Algiers.

project in 1986). A superb resort hotel, a world unto itself with its orange groves and pools, its Moroccan cuisine (third only in refinement to French and Chinese cooking) and gambling, it brought a stream of international celebrities to Marrakech, where the great market has a special exotic appeal because the worlds of Africa and Arabia overlap there.

The *Mamounia* started as an elaborate guest-house in the 16th century, when a sheik built three pavilions in an oasis for distinguished visitors. The great hotel was erected when France colonized Morocco in 1912. The French line, CompagnieTransatlantique, spared no expense in creating an establishment that would be a magic carpet, attracting an international set for parties that lasted for·days or even weeks. Winston Churchill wintered here (and did some of his best paintings). So did Coco Chanel and Josephine Baker, Edith Piaf and Maria Callas. In the *Mamounia*, no one ever succumbed to the tourist's paranoia dramatized by Jimmy Stewart and Doris Day in the Marrakech scenes in *The Man Who Knew Too Much*. In Algeria, too, the Compagnie Transatlantique, strove for all the pleasures of home in their exotic hotels, bringing Alexandre Dumaine, the great chef, to manage their kitchens there in the 1920s.

Colonial North Africa in the late 1930s had become an exotic Riviera, where international celebrities spent "the season" or even settled in semi-permanent residence. In Tunisia, Baron Rudolph d'Erlanger attracted great house parties to Sidi Bou Said, the picturesque hilltop village near the capital. His minaretted Arab palace, an architectural jewel, was typical of the fashion for wedding Eastern motifs with European comfort.

Many hotels in the prewar years imitated this Arabesque idea, usually less successfully than Baron d'Erlanger. The patrician *Saint-Georges*, on the heights of Algiers, counted on the appeal of its handsome gardens and Moorish decor to outdraw the city's main hotel, the *Aletti,* a downtown bloc where politicians gathered and businessmen stayed.

The single grandiose architectural achievement in the region was the striking, modern hotels built in post-independence Algeria by Fernand Pouillon, a revolutionary French architect whose designs were inspired by the vaulted and domed palaces of the Berber tradition in the North African mountains. Constructed along the Mediterrenean outside Algiers, the hotels were mainly used by the government to house visiting delegations during conferences in Algiers. They never attracted many guests, and most have now been turned into apartment buildings. The golden hordes of tourists seeking fun and sun cannot co-exist with the increasingly Islamic austerity of the former French colonies.

THE VOYAGE TO INDIA

British travellers often discovered the Middle East on their way east to India. The word "posh" originated as the acronym stamped on liner tickets of demanding passengers who insisted on travelling "Port Out, Starboard Home" to stay on the cool side of the ship. With the Suez Canal open, most passengers dropped the old habit of disembarking at Alexandria and proceeding via Cairo in coaches or trains and then on to Suez on the Red Sea. Instead, they stayed aboard, looking out at the newly important towns that sprang up along the canal: raffish Port Said, where ships nosed into the canal from the Mediterranean, and Port Suez at the waterway's southern end. Only a handful of passengers ventured into the fetid streets of these waterside towns, and "posh" was hardly the word for the rudimentary, ramshackle accommodations that sprang up in these tropical ports.

Most ships called at Aden, the British possession at the southern tip of Arabia. Essentially a coaling station, the liners and troop ships would anchor off Steamer Point, often for more than a day. Many passengers ventured ashore to sample the comforts of the *Crescent Hotel*, which outranked even the governor-general's palace as the most imposing building in the tiny outpost. Visiting it after the Marxist revolution in what had become South Yemen, I found it remarkably well preserved. A major change was that most staff-members were charged with the task of spying on the guests, not waiting on them. One slept in the hall on the doormat of my room so that the door would awaken him if I tried to go out alone. (Similarly in Syria, a porter was assigned to sleep between my room and that of my Arab woman companion. After outwitting them to reach her room by soaping the squeaky door hinges, I was tiptoeing back to my room an hour before dawn when a nearby cannon was fired to awaken the faithful in time to eat before daybreak so as to observe the Ramadan fast. It woke the watchman. The adventure cost me $25 in hush-money — and the porter then tried to force his way into her room to enjoy whatever the infidel had left).

The final hour of glory of this route came with the prewar flying-boats that plied between Britain and the Far East, stopping in the Persian Gulf island, Bahrain, on the clippers' five-day odyssey to Australia. *Speedbird House* where BOAC overnighted guests and crew, was rudimentary but clublike because of Bahrain's comparatively permissive attitudes. It was the ancestor of the *Gulf Hotel* built there when Gulf Airways was formed by the local states: since the Gulf Air stewardesses stayed there between flights, the *Gulf Hotel* was the scene of raucous parties and room-hopping that were a parody of the old colonial romps.

IN THE HOLY LAND WITH THOMAS COOK

In Palestine, travel had always been more spartan. While people went to Egypt for health or pleasure, Palestine drew mostly Christian pilgrims. They had been coming in limited numbers since the 13th century, usually staying in monasteries, and carving their names on wooden doors, even in medieval times. Franciscan monks operated a chain of hostels, one at each stopover on the pilgrim circuit. In the late 19th century the Franciscans opened separate, lay facilities. One hostel, the *Casa Nova*, had a vaulted cellar dining room which is still a favourite of teachers and young people in Jerusalem. German Kaiser Wilhelm's spectacular pilgrimage through Palestine and Syria in 1898 focused the world's attention on the Holy Land. With improved transportation, pilgrimages had already been increasing in size and many prosperous Victorian travellers chose to use the services of Thomas Cook. Cook, a temperance movement worker who started out in Great Britain organizing railway "day-trips" as a distraction for non-drinkers, found the Holy Land ideal for his type of development, providing comfortable camping arrangements. Servants would precede a party of travellers to the evening campsite, who after a day of sketching, touring and picnicking would arrive in time for bath in large copper tubs and a hot dinner before retiring in floored, blue-cloth tents.

Interior gardens at the *American Colony*, Jerusalem.

What is today Jerusalem's most gracious and comfortable old hotel, the *American Colony*, also began its career about this time. The hotel building, which was originally the palace of a 19th-century pasha, sits in a small garden a few minutes' walk from the Old City. In the upstairs salon, a midnight-blue dome marks the spot where the pasha sat to receive visitors in audience. The older parts of the building are insulated by walls six feet thick and, above the ceilings, a three-foot layer of pottery jars. Drinking water is kept cool in stone jugs with weighted handkerchiefs over the mouths to keep out dirt. It is graceful, picturesque, refined. For generations, it was run by the Vester family, who went out to Jerusalem at the end of the 19th century after a series of personal tragedies and, with other American expatriates, formed a kind of commune. This "American Colony" found itself taking in paying guests and gradually evolved into what became the city's most sophisticated hotel, with a reputation that has spread far beyond the Middle East. Many have tried to write about it,

but its elusive special quality is the hotel's close links with the community around it. In Jerusalem, diplomats and correspondents, Arabists, archaeologists and writers forgather at the *American Colony*. Continuous management by the same family throughout this century has given the hotel an assured identity. The staff have always been Palestinians, many of whom have practically grown up with the hotel, and the Vesters won a place for themselves as people attached to the city regardless of political vicissitudes. During the Turkish retreat from the city in the face of the advancing British in 1919, the Ottoman commander left his wounded at the *American Colony*, confident they would be protected. Looking for a white flag for the actual surrender, the Vester of the day used a bed sheet from the hotel.

The *American Colony* was always cozy and intimate and Arab-oriented in contrast to the towering block across the Holy City — the *King David*. Throughout the inter-war years of the British Mandate in Palestine, the *King David*

Christmas 1896 at the *American Colony,* Jerusalem.

Entrance Hall of the *King David,* Jerusalem, 1980s.

was the focus of Biblical tourism, with international-class facilities and service. It also functioned as an annex of the government and the British army. When Jewish terrorists of Irgun, the underground group led by Menachem Begin (later prime minister of the state of Israel), smuggled milk cans packed with explosives into the kitchens of the busy establishment, the attack was allegedly aimed at the British military. But the carnage — ensured by the short warning of only a few minutes — brought Jewish demands to the attention of a stunned world with brutal force.

Travel, managed by the ubiquitous Thomas Cook, who had first visited the Holy Land in 1857, spread from Jerusalem into the deserts of what was to become Jordan. On the road to Jericho, where the Jordan River flows past the spot where John the Baptist is believed to have baptized Jesus, *khans* and then small inns appeared in the last century to accommodate pilgrims, many of them Russian Orthodox retracing the holy steps on foot. Across the river, tourism consisted mainly of Moslem pilgrims heading south to Mecca (where Thomas Cook had facilities for helping mainly Indian Moslems make the *hajj,* as the pilgrimage to the founding spot of Islam is known). Cooks soon discovered the beauties of Petra, the rose-rock Nabetean city in a hidden valley in the deserts where Lawrence of Arabia would operate later. Early this century, Cook's camp opened, perched among the monumental ruins and partly dug into the cliff face for cool comfort. Eventually, Cook's were bought out by an enterprising Palestinian family, the Nazzals, former travel guides, who today, in their fifth generation in the tourist business, run the *Commodore Hotel* in Beirut, the last hotel operating in the war-ravaged Arab half of the Lebanese capital.

BEIRUT
SPLENDOUR AND DECADENCE

Many of the earliest hotels were started by former dragomans — local entrepreneurs who made all the arrangements for a traveller's trip. Throughout the Ottoman Empire many of the dragomans were Greeks. The *Angleterre Hotel* in Constantinople (Istanbul), long the Ottoman capital's leading establishment, was owned and operated by Missouli, the Greek who had served as a dragoman for the British writer William Kinglake. In Beirut, Nicolas Bassoul started his hotel after gaining a reputation as dragoman to another English traveller, Eliot

Postcard of the *Pera Palace,* Istanbul.

Warburton, whose books were even greater best-sellers than Kinglake's. The new hoteliers were lavishly written up in the famous travel books authored by their customers — the best form of advertising at the time.

This early form of tourism developed first in Constantinople, the capital and court of the Sublime Porte. Foreign visitors needed separate accommodations and help with everyday life. The early "factories" where foreigners lived by nationality (as they did in Persia, on the distant eastern flank of the Moslem world), gradually gave way to rudimentary hotels and more freedom of movement for travellers and later tourists. The best-known survivor of the 19th-century hotels is the *Pera Palace*, with its soft wooden floors and spare furnishings. It speaks volumes about the early hotels' role, as halfway houses which local people viewed as only barely respectable, that Ataturk, the military commander turned ruler and modernizer of Turkey, used the *Pera Palace* for the kind of private debauchery which amused him.

These early hotel arrangements in the Middle East were most clearly evident at Beirut's *Bassoul*, which has now been engulfed with the rest of the waterfront in Lebanon's civil war. When I knew it, the *Bassoul* was a dark, small inn on the palm-lined Avenue des Français. Already bereft of the gardens that used to stretch down to the sea, the stone building had ample proportions — and stunning memories. An unusual early traveller who left his impressions of 19th-century hotels was the American merchant sailor, and later author, Herman Melville. The journal of his Middle East trip in 1857 shows a wanderer's sensitivity to hotel life. He recorded being comfortable at *Bassoul's* which a contemporary description admitted was "wanting in many comforts to which an English traveller is accustomed, but considered the best in Syria" (as the whole region was known then). Melville had been overwhelmed by *Shepheard's*: "The magnitude of *Shepheard's*, lofty ceilings, stone floors, iron beds, thin mattress, no feathers, blinds, mosquito curtains — all showing the tropics. And that you are in the East is shown by fresh dates on table for dessert, cool water in stone jars; waited on by Arab dragomen; clap your hands for servants ... a brilliant scene!"

The *Bassoul* dated from the early days of Beirut's seaside "hotel district", where visitors could move straight from the landing stage to their hotels (rather than cross a city of narrow, congested streets). Nicolas Bassoul had run a *locanda* (an Italian word that in those days covered everything from a pension to a hotel) before he built his famous *Grand Hôtel d'Orient* that eventually was to be known by his own name. It was Thomas Cook's original headquarters in the region, patronized by early Cook's tourist groups in the 1860s. As European-style hotels sprang up (including the *Deutscher Hof*, behind the *Bassoul*, where Bavarian ale was served on an open-air terrace), the district became the centre of Beirut's entertainment district. Next to the *Bassoul*, for example, was the *Normandy*: very much a 1920s relic, its walls and columns were encrusted with millions of tiny square mirrors, like a set left over from a Busby Berkely movie extravaganza. One of its last famous guests was Kim Philby, the Russian double-agent who had remained a loyal customer since he stayed there on his first trip to the Middle East to visit

The *Saint-George,* Beirut, 1940s.

51

Interior of the *Victoria Hotel,* Damascus, 1880.

his famous father, H. St. John Philby, the explorer and the man who, out of spite towards his native Britain, arranged for the oil concessions of Saudi Arabia to go to U.S. majors. Philby actually spent most of his time at another hotel, the *Saint-Georges,* whose well-known bar was his favourite (and he was something of a connoisseur). He was last seen outside Russia in the bar, which for decades in this century became the legendary setting for the finest in Middle East intrigue and pleasure-seeking.

The *Saint-Georges,* like Beirut, was as French in style as Cairo was British. In French-mandated Lebanon, local society mingled with French officers and officials at the *Saint-Georges Hôtel* in an aura of plush serenity which had largely vanished from France. The leading social rendezvous of prewar Beirut was a Sunday afternoon *thé dansant,* on the celebrated terrace overlooking the St. Georges Bay and the Lebanese

mountains in the distance. The Levant coast did not have an opulent tourist season such as Egypt's, but the *Saint-Georges* — built in 1932 as the first in the area on par with the best existing European facilities of the day — offered a degree of comfort and convenience which attracted business from the beginning. It went from strength to strength as Beirut emerged as the Middle East's commercial and communications centre, and became the best-known hotel in the eastern Mediterranean.

The *Saint-Georges* was also one of Beirut's outstanding buildings, architecturally. It was designed by a young Lebanese named Antoine Tabet, who served his apprenticeship in the ateliers of Auguste Perret, during the years in which the French masterbuilder pioneered the use of ferroconcrete, the material which made possible much of modern architecture. The hotel was Tabet's first commission when he returned home. His bold use of raw concrete — in strong, simple rhythms reflecting both a severe functionalism and a feeling for Arab forms — shows the confidence of true modernism.

Although much of the hotel's grandeur departed when the bedrooms were cut down to their present cubicle-like proportions in 1948, the *Saint-Georges* remained renowned for many things: its unmatched location, rich cuisine and discreet service made it one of the world's great hotels. Its atmosphere was described by the British writer Laurie Lee in London's *Sunday Times Colour Magazine*: "Especially at lunchtime, it is Beirut's centre of business and rumour, of brief encounters and social display. Oilmen, government officials, conmen and journalists of all nations — all gather here at midday to taste ... Beirut's simmering sense of affairs. Nubile, bikini-wrapped oil-girls, with figures like greyhounds and waists as pliant as a bundle of banknotes, inhale and exhale their exquisite physical presences up and down the sunspotted terraces."

The *Saint-Georges'* style was incarnate in its suave, unflappable chief concierges, who could solve any problem, manage a guest's shopping and touring, keep any confidence — or often betray it for the right price or reason. Every capital has a hotel to which journalists mysteriously gravitate; the reasons are never satisfactorily explained, but more often than not the secret attraction is the concierge. The *Saint-Georges* was no exception. Concierges there were known to take copies of one reporter's story to send to the paper of a colleague too drunk to be able to file, with just enough editing to keep the inebriated correspondent's style — and job.

When Western journalists covering the anti-Palestinian guerilla drive by the Bedouin troops of Jordan's King Hussein in September 1970 were penned up in the *Intercontinental Hotel* in Amman, despatches were sent in "pooled" batches to the *Saint-Georges* — with justifiable confidence that the concierge would file them correctly and keep the bill until the reporters returned.

The *Saint-Georges'* last day dawned when the wars between Palestinian guerillas and local groups reached Beirut in the mid-1970s. At what proved to be the final meal, a colleague and I lunched with the American ambassador by the sea with only one other person on the enclosed terrace, a Lebanese member of Parliament whose father had been president of the country. Cosily sheltered by the hotel from the escalating street fighting, we were laughing at the American ambassador's worldly-wise refusal to get excited about "a war so small they don't even have airpower" — when the first bullets started thudding into the walls. As we left hastily, the Lebanese politician was on the phone to the Palestinian guerilla chief Yasser Arafat, screaming, "This

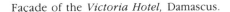

Façade of the *Victoria Hotel,* Damascus.

The *Shah Abbas,* Ispahan, 1970.

hotel is my club! Tell your men to stop it." Within minutes the hotel was captured by Christian militia men, who joined my colleague who had stayed behind in drinking up as much as they could of the hotel's excellent cellar. Within days, the hotel had been fought over so much that it was beyond restoration, and it remained a blackened hulk (testimony to the builder's structural genius) for years.

The *Saint-Georges* was architecturally and professionally of international calibre. With 90 rooms, it was the biggest hotel of its time in Lebanon or Syria. But smaller, earlier hotels had strong personalities, still perceptible to travellers today. The *Palmyra Hotel* in Baalbek, built in the same reddish limestone as the majestic Roman ruins there, has bathtubs (installed in 1924) which are so long that the tallest guest can stretch out full length in the steaming water. On winter mornings, you could wipe the condensation off the high French doors of each room's balcony and see the celebrated columns of Baalbek silhouetted against the sun-reddened, time-rutted flanks of Mount Lebanon. Built in 1875 by a Greek from Istanbul, the *Palmyra* was Lebanon's first Western-style hotel. Baalbek was already a tourist attraction but, more important, it was the first day's stage by diligence from Damascus.

The *Palmyra* was built above a Roman theatre, its garden peopled with statuary, and its fortunes rose in the 1960s with Baalbek's world-renowned summer festivals of music and theatre. The brilliant "soirées" in the *Palmyra*

after Baalbek "premières" enhanced the hotel's sense of belonging to the place.

SYRIAN INTERLUDE

Two Syrian hotels have survived from that period — the *Baron* in Aleppo and the *Zenobia* in the ruined city of Palmyra.

Hotels in Aleppo, the bustling commercial capital of Syria, were virtually a monopoly of Armenians. From father to

Author William Saroyan leaving the *Bacon's.*

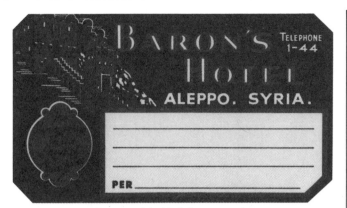

Baggage-label of the *Baron's*.

son, they passed down a tradition of speaking several languages and the gestures that come with a meticulous host: slippers await the guests in every room so that they need not track in street dirt.

The two Mazloumian brothers had made money operating a small Aleppo hotel, the *Ararat*, but, early in this century, they thought the city was ready for something new — a truly palatial hotel. In its day, their *Baron Hotel* was an establishment of unheard-of splendour. The architect was French; concrete was used for the first time in Aleppo; workmen were brought from Egypt; there was a bathroom on both floors. (The only concession to practicality was the name "Baron", not a title, simply the Armenian word for "mister" — which is easy to pronounce in any language). The Mazloumians' gamble paid off. The hotel was barely completed when the First World War broke out. The Turkish commander-in-chief, Jamal Pasha, took over the *Baron* as his headquarters, and his lavish entertainment started the hotel's reputation. Near the end of the war, when the Turks unleashed a series of Armenian pogroms, only Jamal's intervention saved the Mazloumians from deportation or worse. The victorious British commander, General Allenby, eventually used the *Baron* as his headquarters, and Emir Faisal, leader of the Arab revolt aided by T.E. Lawrence, reviewed Allied troops from the balcony of his room. When peace was restored, the Turks returned as civilians, including Ataturk: the room he stayed in is kept unchanged because so many Turkish guests still ask to see it.

Perhaps the hotel's most interesting early guest was Lawrence, who periodically moved to the *Baron* for a rest after the rigours of nearby Carchemish, where he was busily engaged in archaeology and spying. In a letter he said, "You can see what style I'm enjoying," a cryptic reference explained by the *Baron Hotel* stationery he was writing on, which had a drawing of the hotel printed at the top of each sheet. Koko Mazloumian, who managed the hotel until nationalization, also remembers Gene Tunney suddenly appearing one snowy night: the American boxer

had been staying in Beirut to welcome the cars on the "Citroën Expedition" to China, and he had heard the *Baron* still had a stock of a rare French vintage, so he came to buy it.

Palmyra had been the stage for larger-than-life heroines since the Empress Zenobia proclaimed her desert kingdom. Lady Hester Stanhope, a forceful romantic of the 18th century, claimed Bedouin tribes crowned her "Queen of the Desert" there. The *Hotel Zenobia*, still standing on the sand in the heart of the imposing ruins, also has its woman. It was built and run by the Baroness d'Andurin, a personable, strong-willed French noblewoman, whose career in Syria — and graceful touch as a hotel manager — gathered a rich aura of scandal. The main bedroom has a gallery where the Baroness, peering down through a spyhole, could keep an eye on things without breaking the local taboo on women appearing in public. Today, staying at the *Zenobia* involves braving indifferent service and brackish plumbing (tainted by the sulphurous stench of the oasis water) noticed by authoress Agatha Christie Mallowan when she stayed there with her archaeologist husband.

King Gustave Adolphe and Queen Louise of Sweden followed by Prince Bertil entering the *Baron's*.

EPILOGUE

PERSIA

The politico-cultural animosity that ultimately buried the hotels of Lebanon also spread to the region's largest country, non-Arab Iran. Proud of his nation's Persian heritage, Reza Shah (father of the Shah overthrown by Ayatollah Khomeini) constructed a chain of *Ramsar Hotels* in the 1930s that were the backbone of social life along the caviar-rich Caspian Sea. One of these was so handsome that the Shah, as a young man, commandeered it for use as his northern palace.

But nowhere in Iran could match the rich, intact architectural heritage of Ispahan, the nation's garden city, far south of dusty Tehran. Ispahan was the site of the Middle East's most ambitious modern attempt to recreate the old palaces when, in the late 1960s, the Shah's government built the glittering *Shah Abbas,* a luxury hotel converted from a cavernous *khan*. Many of us preferred the old prewar *Irantour*, with its seedy bar, which felt as if it belonged in a thriller by Graham Greene.

But the disappearance of both, in Khomeini's Islamic Republic, removed the last remnants of the era.

Baggage-label, 1930s.

ALL THE FABLES

OF THE EAST

by Anthony Lawrence

Hotels in Southeast Asia range in unimaginable variety from gleaming palaces to bungalows up jungle-tracks, with corrugated-iron roofs. But they have usually shared one inestimable advantage over the non-Asian world — the quality of the people who work in them. Southeast Asia is traditionally a place where even the simplest villagers are endowed with good manners and goodwill towards strangers and have never expected much in the way of high wages. This meant that a large reservoir of human talent was already there waiting to be recruited, when the era of Grand Hotels dawned in the Far East.

This chapter began, broadly speaking, with the opening of the Suez Canal in 1869. The Grand Hotel was essentially a Western type of institution and in pre-Canal days the need for it was limited. Those who journeyed out from Europe were mostly colonial officials, troops needed for garrison duty or local wars, and ships' crews; and all of them had their own accommodation of varying kinds. When the journey from Europe was dramatically shortened by the cutting of the Canal and the new big steamships brought out wives and families, tourists and businessmen, the hotel scene began to change. Slowly at first but then (as local entrepreneurs saw the possibilities of catering for a moneyed clientèle) with growing enthusiasm and investment. European architects came out for high fees to face-lift older buildings, French chefs were hired to add flavour to the cooking, Swiss managers installed to train the staff.

This was the time between the late nineteenth century and the Second World War. Travellers basked in the luxury of the big ships of the Messageries Maritimes, the P & O, Hapag-Lloyd, Lloyd-Triestino, and the Dutch KPM. And upon disembarkation they settle into the comfort of the hotel with its plush public rooms, its orchestras at teatime, its long bars, large bedrooms with ceiling fans and broad verandahs, and silent, respectful servants.

After the Second World War came radical changes which were to have an impact on the mode of travel and travelling pattern. As air travel developed, big passenger ships decreased in number; and air-conditioning was beginning to make life more bearable for Westerners who had to endure the tropic heat. Malaria still lurked in the countryside and cholera was still a recurring menace in some of the cities, but the well-protected Westerner ran little risk.

The Far East was becoming more accessible, and a healthier place for sojourns or visits, but at the same time it was losing something of its mystery.

The Westerners themselves had changed. The wealthy tourists who came were soon joined by others with smaller means as well as by teachers, technicians and advisers financed by international bodies and government aid schemes. Often the work of this latter group would take them away from the capitals to more provincial areas as yet untouched by modern conveniences.

The big city hotels had to serve the needs of politicians, businessmen and journalists. For the businessman entertaining clients or the journalist reporting the political scene, the state of the hotel's efficiency could well make the difference between success and failure. Their choice of hotels were invariably those where messages were faithfully transmitted, where the manager had contacts with the airlines and where taxis would arrive within minutes. They avoided the places where travellers cheques were likely to be lost or stolen and where the cuisine was expensive and second-rate.

Nowadays modern hotel facilities — it seems almost a revolution in standards of service — are pretty much taken for granted in the cities. The mosquito nets have vanished

Façade of the *Strand,* Rangoon, 1980.

along with the mosquitoes, the water from the taps is safe to drink, the salads are safe to eat, and faint, indefinable odours no longer rise from dark lift-shafts. Tourism — that mass transportation of humans by 'plane and bus-load, with promise of exotic scenery and local dances, edible food and adequate hygiene', is the quick and decisive sterilizing influence.

Yet something has been lost along the way, along with the neighbourliness and intimacies of long journeys by sea before the airlines came. There is a sameness among many of the fine new hotels — the same huge hall, the atrium, rising many storeys high to the glass roof, with all the rooms reached by interior balconies; the observation lifts with their bird's-eye view of the great lounges below; the well-trained smiling staff who repeat the American-style greeting of "Have a Nice Day" even at ten o'clock at night; the reliable menus which rarely include the more exotic fruits; and the sumptuous interior decoration in a mixture of styles.

Thirty years ago when the hotel revolution was in its earlier stages, some of the famous older hotels were going through a difficult time. They were losing staff to the newcomers who were attracting the new tourist trade. It does not help that great men have made a hotel famous if the wallpaper is starting to peel and the coffee tastes of black earth. The package-tour companies were sometimes avoiding well-known names apart from the one-meal visit; they took their clients to the more modern hotels. The old and famous soon awoke to this situation: managements were changed, new policies followed, public relations campaigns initiated. History and famous traditions were now an added selling point in a good hotel's appeal.

It came as a surprise to me, a radio correspondent arriving in Singapore in the autumn of 1956, to be driven by his welcoming hosts to the *Cathay* and not to a world-famous hotel. It was an unforgettable first night in the Far East. The air-conditioner roared faintly as if the flight from London were being prolonged in a dream-world in that stone-walled monastic room. When I got up for the third time and turned off the machine to get some quiet I soon lay soaked in sweat and awoke next morning robbed of strength, as though a fever had just subsided. The reviving factor was the Chinese room-boy, polite, smiling, communicating in pidgin-English, who brought breakfast, newspaper and strong tea, and who collected the laundry.

There were no radio or television in a hotel room in those days. Keeping abreast of events was not an easy task. I soon learned that foreign correspondents were in the habit of frequenting a hotel called the *Cockpit* and there I transferred the same afternoon. The *Cockpit* still exists in Singapore but in a new building no longer recognizable by former habitués. Back in 1956 it still retained the shape of the old colonial residence it had formerly been, with an imposing porch to protect arriving carriages from tropical rain, a panelled entrance hall, and a broad stairway leading up to the main bedrooms. A doctor of our acquaintance, an old Singapore hand, recalled bridge parties in that place when it was still the home of a wealthy local merchant. Then it was run and part-owned by the handsome Mrs Ronnie Hilborne, wife of an English barrister. The garden at the back contained a number of chalets, in one of which dwelt John Ridley of the London *Daily Telegraph*; he spent many of his waking hours presiding over the hotel's bar downstairs, having arranged with a local newspaper journalist to ring him up of any important news.

The bar was a hub of activity: not only local and foreign newsmen would call in there but also public relations people, army officers, businessmen, and acquaintances from other Asian countries. For a while one might enjoy the illusion of covering a large area of the world from this one companionable place, where the very inscriptions printed in flowing italic above the drinks counter, urging the companions to drown any dangerous thirst, seemed

Entrance of the Teutonia Club, 1900.

boldly reassuring. Mr Wong, the earnest maître d'hôtel, would come to announce for the third time that dinner was ready, but we were only halfway through the tale of the Dalai Lama and his visit to India, and how the smart man from the *Mail* had it all written and filed in advance — only that the Dalai Lama didn't turn up. And the man who scooped the world's newspapers with the news of Sukarno's death, but Sukarno hadn't died. The misfortunes of others make the best stories.

Preferred accommodation in the *Cockpit* for a family, after wife and small son arrived, was in two generous rooms over the main lounge and dining hall. The Filipino band, playing for all its worth just below, kept us awake until one o'clock on Saturday nights, but at least we had an enormous bathroom, with a long bath and water-heater. In less sophisticated places you would be lucky to have a shower, or even ladle water from a gigantic jar. The staff were Chinese and Malay and from them we experienced that inborn politeness and readiness to help that we later found so widespread throughout Asia.

Singapore was used as a base for outward bound trips as well as a point of contact with London and the BBC. The local scene had its dramatic aspects — Singapore's march to independence marred by riots and the last of Communist ambushes and attacks up in Malaya — but it was not enough to keep a correspondent dividing his time week after week between the *Cockpit* and his small office in the radio station. Whenever trouble broke out in other Southeast Asian countries London was sure to cable the instruction to go off at once and report it.

Jakarta was my first assignment of this kind — where I had to cover a revolt of discontented colonels. The place to stay, my colleagues had said, was the *Hôtel des Indes* (rechristened the *Duta Indonesia*), but when I arrived it was full. (Many years later, when I managed to book a room there, it appeared strangely run-down and unkempt, a place of gloomy loggias and damp, deserted courtyards). I had to seek refuge instead in the *Robertson's Hotel* (long since vanished), a rambling single-storeyed building not far from the airport. Over a washbasin in the hotel were two notices, one of which read: the tap-water (I was rinsing my teeth in it at the time) must on no account be used in

An interior courtyard at the *Raffles*, 1963.

the mouth; the other warned that the room might have to be vacated in minutes if a plane-load of passengers arrived unexpectedly! I then took an anti-malaria tablet and learned from the bottle's label that one should have started with this at least two days before entering a malarial area. Ten years later the hotel scene was transformed by the opening of the *Hotel Indonesia*, under an excellent Swiss manager. Instead of a test of endurance a news assignment in Indonesia now verged on the enjoyable. The music of gongs, the gamelan, echoed in the great foyer of the hotel. Publicity for the hotel was limited as this was during the period when President Sukarno was embroiled in the power-struggles which would end in his final eclipse — and for months the occupancy rate was thirty per cent. As tourism developed in the 70s, other new hotels followed the *Indonesia*, and the face of downtown Jakarta took on a modern look.

Yet often the mind returns to earlier days. To wake in the dawn to the sound of soft Indonesian voices beyond the verandah, the crowing of cocks and the rustle of palm-branches in the garden — these are some of the simpler pleasures denied the modern traveller, hermetically sealed off from local life. Today the *Robertson's Hotel* is unremembered, its Welsh proprietor had returned to his native land twenty-five years ago, but the sound of the gamelan — even the smell of clove cigarettes — at once recall not only days of anxiety and discomfort but also a sense of living somewhere quite extraordinary, where people led an existence free from the encumbrances of modern living.

After the strain and fatigue of reporting political events and upheavals in other Asian countries it was always an enormous relief to return to friendly faces and familiar rooms in Singapore. By this time the winds of change and

Ballroom of the *E & O*, opened in 1923.

Crag Hotel, Penang Hill, Penang.

independence were blowing strongly and in Kuala Lumpur preparations were underway for the great Merdeka (Freedom) ceremonies of 1957. In those days the Kuala Lumpur hotels included the *Merlin*, the *Majestic* and the *Station*, the latter being part of the unusual Indian-architecture complex of the railway station itself. "It wasn't in the least like any railway station we'd seen before," a new arrival of the 'thirties recalls. "It was designed with domes and small spires and lots of oriental arched windows."

Less noisy, further away from the trains, was the *Majestic Hotel* situated up a hill in the city, where planters came to stay on their visits to Kuala Lumpur. It has survived for many years since, with its ceiling fans, mosquito nets, sustaining western breakfasts in its large dining room, and its elderly faithful staff.

The *Merlin*, one of the fine hotels of Malaysia, is remembered by many correspondents as a refuge and oasis in the grim days of the race riots of 1969, when the hotel management rose heroically to the occasion by providing food and shelter to a motley crowd of frightened refugees. Journalists ventured forth on news-gathering expeditions until the continual menace of a machine-gun thrust through the car-window, and the warning that the safe-conduct issued the night before was now valueless diminished their zeal. That was an unusual experience in a country known for its smiling faces and friendliness. Less testing was a stay in the famous *Eastern and Oriental Hotel* in Penang when the Duke of Edinburgh was paying a visit to the historic settlement. The *E & O* has pleasant gardens reaching to the sea, with old cannons for children to mount, and buffets and barbecues under the stars. Larger, newer hotels have been built but nothing to surpass the *E & O*.

But in 1957 when the Duke of Edinburgh was visiting, the survival of many colonial institutions seemed far from certain. With the British flag lowered on the Kuala Lumpur *padang* on the stroke of a hot August midnight, the way

The Sarkies brothers, from left to right: Tigran, Arshak, Martin and Aviet.

Dolah – Splata itu?
Kassim – *(deciphering with much difficulty)* – Raff-fulls Dolah – Ah, barang kall Tuan Sarkies.

Smith – I'd like to see more of those girls.
Jones – You will, if you go to *Raffles* to night!

was set for Singapore to stage its own elections for self-government. What would become of the white man's clubs and hotels?

Those were days of conflicting loyalties. Some rushed to gain favour with the new regime by running down the old; others hailed independence but still regretted the colonial atmosphere in its more agreeable aspects. There was talk of demolishing the Singapore Cricket Club and some whispered that a place like *Raffles Hotel* could not possibly survive. And yet, just as the statue of Sir Stamford Raffles, founder of Singapore, was allowed to remain in acknowledgement of the territory's past, so the hotel named after him survived; and now it flourishes, a Singapore landmark known to tourists throughout the world.

Although modernized the *Raffles* still retains something of its earlier days — the white facades, the cathedral-like loftiness of the main dining room, the famous long bar and the travellers' palms out in the garden, so called because they are supposed always to turn in the direction of the sun, even when it's hidden, and thus give a rough guide to the wayfarer. And of course the famous drink, the "million-dollar cocktail", a concoction of gin, sweet and dry vermouth, egg white, pineapple juice, and bitters.

The original building was owned as a restaurant by the Dare brothers, sons of a well-known sea-captain who had suffered heavy money losses. In those days (the late 1870s)

it directly overlooked the sea and the Dares were able to sell it at a good price to the Armenian businessmen, the Sarkies brothers. They turned it into a hotel in the 1880s and so the *Raffles* was born. The Sarkies were an energetic lot. Old-timers have recalled that the youngest, Arshak Sarkies, could be seen dancing round the ballroom in the *E & O* with a whisky-and-soda balanced on his head, for a bet. He was a generous man, for when the great slump came in the late 1920s, many planters and tin-miners who had run up large bills in the Sarkies' hotel group had their accounts "overlooked" on his orders, and some in really bad straits were provided with passages home to Britain.

A famous early visitor to the *Raffles* was Rudyard Kipling who arrived in Singapore with friends on the *Madura* on his way to Japan and San Francisco. Of the *Raffles* he wrote: "The food is excellent ... the rooms are bad."

Another visitor, the American mining engineer, Norman Cleaveland, was surprised to find the plumbing at the *Raffles* to be "extremely primitive" with the traditional "thunder-box" instead of flush-toilets. Likewise he was confounded by the famous Shanghai jar which was used for washing — a huge pitcher from which cold water could be ladled. Like many a new arrival in the Far East, Cleaveland thought he was supposed actually to get into this great jar, which he did and found it "a tight fit, but cosy". The Shanghai jar had its good points. Due to evaporation through the porous clay, the water inside always stayed deliciously cold. A man might even keep bottles of beer in it, in days when refrigerators were still unknown.

In 1897 the *Raffles* was extensively renovated which caused it to be called the "Savoy of Singapore" in comparison with the famous London hotel. The centre block was demolished to be replaced by a much larger three-storey block in Renaissance style. A wide decorated verandah ran round all four sides of the building and the magnificent new dining room was paved in Carrara marble. The entire hotel was now lighted with electricity. The Sarkies proudly claimed that facilities at the *Raffles* were "equal to those of any hotel in the East".

Kipling had written earlier: "Feed at the *Raffles* and sleep at the *Europe*."

This latter hotel, a keen competitor, had been built in the early 1830s alongside the Padang, the central grass-covered field fronting the sea. In its heyday before the First World War it seems to have been considered the best hotel in Singapore. Joseph Conrad may well have had the *Europe* in mind when, in the earlier chapters of his famous novel *Lord Jim*, he describes the evening spent with the disgraced young officer who had abandoned his ship and had his certificate cancelled. Conrad gives the hotel the invented title of Malabar House:

"An outward-bound mail-boat had come in that afternoon, and the big dining room of the hotel was more than half full of people with a hundred pounds round-the-world tickets in their pockets. There were married couples looking domesticated and bored with each other in the midst of their travels; there were small parties and large parties ... all just as intelligently receptive of new impressions as their trunks upstairs. The dark-faced servants

The Russian General Stoessel at the *Raffles,* 18 May 1905.

Façade of the *Hôtel Métropole,* Hanoi, 1920.

tripped without noise over the vast and polished floor ..." On the front gallery where Lord Jim and his host adjourn for coffee and cigars, "candles burned in glass globes on little octagon tables; clumps of stiff-leaved plants separated sets of cosy wicker chairs; and between the pairs of columns, whose reddish shafts caught in a long row the sheen from the tall windows, the night, glittering and sombre, seemed to hang like a splendid drapery. The riding lights of ships winked afar like setting stars, and the hills across the roadstead resembled rounded black masses of arrested thunder-clouds."

On the last grand gala night of the *Europe* all Singapore's upper crust were assembled for dinner, including members of the Legislative and Executive Councils. At the top table was the joint chairman of Mansfields (famous Singapore trading house) and the Straits Steamship Company, Charles Wurtzburg. Word came discreetly that a young prince from a Middle East country had come into the dining room with his aide-de-camp. Seats among the notables were at once provided for them. Both young men were most picturesque in their eastern attire and made an agreeable impression. The prince himself smiled and said little but the ADC's English was excellent. In fact they were Bill Dobbs and Robin Isherwood of Mansfields, dressed for a lark. They thought they had got away with it until on Monday morning they were summoned to the boss's office. Wurtzburg had spotted them at once, and they got a dressing down; but that was the end of it.

After its extensive renovations the *Raffles* attracted even more tourists and distinguished visitors; the hotel advertisements boast of generals, ministers, men of wealth and ladies of stage, screen and society. Conrad is not recorded as having ever stayed at the *Raffles*; almost certainly during his very few visits to Singapore as a ship's officer he would have used the officers' quarters at the Seamen's Home.

The *Raffles* was a barometer of Singapore and the world,

Hôtel du Commerce, Haiphong, 1920.

flourishing in days of prosperity, languishing in times of want as during the slump in the rubber and tin markets. The Sarkies brothers fell on hard times and sold out, and the brothers blamed it on the warm-hearted Arshak for his lack of business toughness. However under the new management the hotel soon took centre-stage in that strange colonial society between the wars which, in retrospect, seems so impossibly class-conscious and philistine. *Raffles* became famous for its regular dances, accompanied by bands brought out from Europe. Young men had to wear evening dress on the dance-floor regardless of the equatorial heat, though white jackets were allowed. They danced the waltzes and fox-trots. On the road outside, in the velvety darkness, groups of curious locals watched the couples circulating under the bright lights in what, to Asian minds, seemed a strange and immoral ritual. In any case the management allowed no non-western girl into the hotel (apart from the occasional Eurasian); and any European woman whose profession was in doubt would at once be shipped home.

Rumour has it that during the Second World War, the *Raffles* was a brothel for Japanese officers; but the truth is that it was simply used as an officers' billet, where behaviour was correct. The *Raffles*, unlike other buildings in Singapore used by the dreaded Kempeitai, has no ghost stories dating from the war.

With peace and the return of the British, the hotel soon enjoyed its former prestige again, though now the world was changing. The Far East was no longer a suburb of Europe. Colonial empires were disappearing and the white man no longer called the score wherever he went. Racist attitudes were under attack.

In Singapore the *Raffles* management found themselves restricted in their choice of ballroom dancing; there were regulations against hiring foreign dance bands.

Visitors like Noel Coward or Somerset Maugham stayed in the *Raffles* but regarded the human scene there with a quizzical eye. Coward had already been in Singapore in

late 1929, when he stayed a month; and he was fairly sarcastic in most of what he said and wrote about British colonials as is reflected in his song "Mad Dogs and Englishmen Go Out in the Noonday Sun". He found consolation in the company of a touring company "The Quaints" whom he had met on the voyage out.

"Some of the more refined social lights of Singapore looked obliquely at us, as if we were not quite the thing — a little too rowdy, perhaps, on the common side. I'm sure they were right. Actors always laugh more loudly than other people, when they're enjoying themselves, and we laughed most of the time."

Coward's last visit to the *Raffles* was in 1968, when he stayed in suite number 10.

Somerset Maugham usually occupied suite number 78, and he would write in the garden just outside. For him, he said, the hotel stood for "all the fables of the exotic East". But when he paid his last visit in 1959 (six years before he died) he told an interviewer that the East had changed fundamentally from the time when he first listened to accounts of the daily lives of planters, civil servants and their wives and used this material for his earlier short stories. "Nowadays if things go wrong maritally and domestically," he said, "the wife can fly home to mother in twenty-four hours. In those earlier days Europe was five weeks away by ship and home leave came only after five years. Those were the circumstances that put a strain on peoples' endurance and made them behave unusually."

At the same time, changes were also taking place with the dwindling in the numbers of Dutch and French officials in the East. More locals were taking over government posts and the foreigner was appearing less as a bureaucrat and more in the role of a technical adviser. The colonial powers left varying imprints on the cities and hotels of Southeast Asia. In Indochina the hotels retained a French

Hôtel des Mines, Hon Gay.

style long after the French administration had gone, and their cooking was nearly always better than in places where other imperialists had ruled. The affability of the maître d'hôtel, the room service, the drinks on the *terrasse* — were all reminiscent of a French way of doing things. It matched the colonial rococo charm of Saigon's city hall, streets lined with flame-of-the-forest trees and the small formal parks.

The hotels of Vietnam, Cambodia and Laos are closely associated in the minds of foreign journalists with a seemingly interminable news-story spread over two decades of politics, terrorism, assassination and unrestricted warfare. Only a handful of visitors and former administra-

Façade of the *Hôtel Mottet*, Cap St-Jacques, c. 1910.

tors, nearly all of them French, can recall earlier colonial times, when plantation owners would come into Saigon for relaxation and amusement, or visitors from the West, arriving in the grand white steamers of the Messageries Maritimes, stayed for a few days before game hunting in the provinces or continuing their world tour to Shanghai and Yokohama.

Soon after the Second World War began the complicated series of events that would end with the catastrophe of Dien Bien Phu; then a pause before dry rot set in again, leading to a war that would end with the American retreat from Indochina and the fall of Saigon.

During that pause in the late '50s Indochina wore an appearance of tranquillity but deep ominous rumbles were stirring. Yet it did seem to some that Ngo Dinh Diem, the American-approved mandarin, might manage to survive in South Vietnam despite the influence of his brother Nhu and Nhu's vivacious but much hated wife. Saigon wore an air of uneasy tension in the summer heat, but optimists were not lacking. The tourists had not returned but the café *terrasses* needed no protective grilles, markets

were thronged, business seemed to be picking up and the government was talking about land reform to ease the life of the peasants.

The business visitor was advised to stay in the *Majestic* down by the riverside; it was large and well run and, unlike the *Continental Palace* further up the Rue Catinat, had a reasonably efficient telephone installation. The *Continental* was comfortable but old-fashioned; its rooms resembled large monastic cells giving on to balconies framed in bougainvillea. It was a place for calm thought rather than organizing interviews and deals.

By the early '60s the scene had changed. President Diem, persuaded by his American advisers, had hired a Madison Avenue public relations man to project a dynamic image of the regime. Foreign correspondents were suddenly most welcome and when they arrived for the conducted tours and briefings they found a fine new hotel across the square from the *Continental*. This was the *Caravelle*, resplendent in its pale blue decor, air-conditioned throughout, with blue cotton sheets on the beds. It could really be called an international class hotel. One might even enjoy the doubtful luxury of listening to a quartet of bored-looking western musicians in the large dining room upstairs. It was a place for official cocktail parties and diplomatic receptions and it seemed to herald a re-birth for Saigon, a new beginning, watched with growing interest by the rest of the outside world.

From this time onwards many foreign news bureaus established their offices in the *Caravelle*, and for years senior American army visitors would stay there. But by now the *Continental* had been modernized to some extent and there were telephones in the bedrooms. A more human atmosphere prevailed there, due partly to the stocky, overweight ever-smiling manager Mr. Loi and the proprietor Philippe Franchini, a Corsican who was also an artist and a painter, who exhibited his works in the restaurant attached to the hotel, the Dolce Vita. The *Continental* had also become famous for its outside *terrasse*, raised several feet above the pavement, and which was known to all as the Continental Shelf. Everyone came here for drinks and talks; and here the correspondent would find colleagues, officials, foreign diplomats, soldiers, visitors from international institutions, whores and hangers-on of all kinds. It was for many years the great place to rendezvous; and somehow its character was peculiar to itself, disconnected from the rest of the hotel. The *terrasse* was a centre of rumour, unsubstantiated claims, downright lies and general hubbub. The hotel itself was more of an oasis, where a man could hear himself think.

The design and arrangements of the *Continental* never ceased to intrigue. The great double doors, resembling the entrance to a French country house and which open until midnight, led directly into the lobby where elderly Vietnamese were forever adding columns of dongs (piastres) with scratchy steel-nibbed pens. After registering, the guest would be led to an open-cage lift manned by a lively little boy in page's uniform, reminiscent of the time of the Belle Époque. It gave a warning rattle as it passed the first floor, as if the fittings were working loose. Why, besides the lift were there two separate staircases, one of which leads only up into a cul-de-sac? It seemed that many years ago the hotel had been smaller, until it took over the building next door but had never bothered to remove the extra stairs. Dim corridors thinly carpeted stretched into the gloom; and there were galleries looking down on an inner garden, a gravelled path imitation of a Montagnard village with thatched roof bowers and flowering bushes. Guests took breakfast there, sometimes alarmed by a fierce peacock strutting up and down; and behind it a tank of green water held a huge fish with barely enough room to turn. Both in time disappeared, probably eaten by guests at one of those wedding feasts in which the *Continental* specialized.

Verandah of the *Continental*, Saigon.
from a publicity brochure.

In the afternoons the inner retreats of the hotel were blanketed in a great silence. All Saigon closed down for a long siesta at midday and came to life again only four hours later. In the corners of hallways room-boys lay on the floor in the deepest of sleep, as though they were dead; throughout the whole building there was not a sound, not even a clinking of glass or the swish of a broom. It was as if the whole world had stopped breathing.

For a correspondent reporting the war the *Continental* was a strangely reassuring place to return to after tense excursions into the countryside, and sometimes a feeling of relief at having survived a close shave would be mixed with the bodily fatigue experienced at day's end. The bath filled slowly but at last all the dirt and sweat would be washed off. Then in fresh clean clothes down to the restaurant for a *poulet à l'estragon* and Dalat strawberries, washed down with a red wine whose quality has worsened over the years but was drinkable almost to the last.

Of the origins of the *Continental* perhaps only Philippe Franchini could tell the full story — how after passing through various hands it was bought by his father, Mathieu Franchini, a young Corsican teacher. Mathieu was to become a kind of uncrowned king of the Saigon world and underworld, a general go-between for men on secret missions, bosses of the drug traffic and manipulators of business. He faded from the scene when the French gave up Vietnam.

Philippe carried on, maintaining in the *Continental* a web of extensive relationships. He was a man of taste and sensibility, a friend of correspondents, and the symbol of the good hotelier. His willing instruments were M. Loi the manager or major-domo, and the severe and correct housekeeper or *gouvernante*. The very sight of her in the distance galvanized room-boys into anxious movement. She would inquire of a guest in her clipped French whether everything was in order, as a kind of daily greeting. Any complaints were dealt with efficiently at breakneck speed.

Newsmen covering the Vietnam War measured the ups and downs of its course by the fortunes of the hotel. When the government decided to counterbalance all the evil things written about Saigon by carrying out a thorough clean-up of its black marketeers, illegal moneychangers, pimps and prostitutes, a regular occupant of an upstairs room might suddenly find himself with a visitor — a smart girl in an *ao-dai* who in incomprehensible Vietnamese would appear to be apologizing for her presence while insisting on staying — for just a little while. This would be one of the girls from the *terrasse* or the street, with no other immediate intention but to dodge the police net.

And later in the war when tempers grew short, and anti-government demonstrators were fiercely handled, the *Continental* itself came under attack when soldiers came

In front of the *Majestic,* Saigon, July 1955.

searching for a man who had gone out of his way to defy them. They lobbed tear-gas cannisters and the stench of gas hung about the corridors and public rooms. It really seemed then as if the end of an era had come.

What has become of it all? What had happened to the stern *gouvernante,* and M. Loi? They appeared as if they had vanished down the corridors of the old hotel. In fact, after the Communists took over Saigon, M. Loi had to face accusations from fellow waiters and was greatly humiliated. He was later seen looking haggard and moving with the aid of a walking-stick. The *Continental* became a hostel for North Vietnamese officers and officials, and the few remaining foreigners had to leave.

More recently however, tourists as well as veterans of the war were allowed to revisit Saigon. They reported that the *Continental* was now a place of darkness, locked up and deserted, with the grilles drawn across the Continental Shelf.

One man who was spared the nightmare of the final collapse in Saigon was the proprietor of the *Hôtel Royal,* a quiet old man with courtly manners and the crumpled chalk-white face of the opium addict. He was a Corsican and his name was Ottavi. He received the Order of the Legion of Honour during his final illness, and died shortly before the collapse of Saigon.

Freelance journalists of limited means would stay at the *Royal* for its rooms were far cheaper than those at the *Caravelle* or the *Continental.* But though the services offered were basic and the rooms rather cramp, the cooking was sometimes excellent. French-speaking correspondents liked to call in for dinner and converse with old Ottavi and his lively Vietnamese wife.

"He is down to five pipes a day," she told me one evening in early 1969. "He did give it up altogether for some days, but then his legs swelled alarmingly and he was taken off to hospital in a semi-coma. When he recovered he at once began smoking again.

"The nuisance is that," she went on, "the opium is simply not pure. The traffickers adulterated it in a quite shocking way, and so M. Ottavi is always having trouble with his insides. He ought to settle back in his native Corsica but his other 'wife' won't let him. I mean the opium. You know the opium story? There was this ugly daughter whom nobody would ask for her hand in marriage, so she decided on suicide and declared that from her grave a plant would spring which men, when once they touched it, would never be able to leave it alone again but would always cling to it like a wife. And that is opium. Of course," she added, "I am not saying this actually happened; it is what I have heard people say."

Ottavi would talk of the bygone days when he had been in charge of the dining room at the *Majestic* and the French were everywhere in Vietnam. They even did menial jobs, like driving trams. The Americans were different but still they were also to fail in the War. Frankly he found their mentality impossible to understand. How was the dinner? Quite satisfactory? His gentle voice seemed to echo from the past. He had come to own a sizable hotel business in Saigon at one time but his partner had died, leaving three widows and twenty children and the property had to be split up among them. One widow took the *Hôtel Catinat,* another now had the *Hotel des Nations* which had in fact been part of the *Royal.* While he was telling the head waiter to bring us each another cognac, an explosion from across the river, part of some night operation, rattled the windows behind us.

A year before Saigon fell I went to the *Royal* one evening to find the dining room almost deserted. M. Ottavi came slowly and tremblingly from the shadows. Rumour had it that because of the fighting the opium suppliers had failed him. He told me sadly that he was very ill indeed, suffering from swelling of the limbs, rheumatism "and other things."

Larger-than-life abrasive personalities came and went on the Saigon scene during those years — generals, ministers, important news commentators, TV stars. It is difficult, now, to recall even their names. Yet the coconut matting along the corridors of the *Royal,* the half-empty dining room and the gentlemanly stooping figure of old Ottavi remain fresh in one's memory.

Vietnam was not the only country of Indochina to drift into the turbulence of political upheaval. The 60's also saw the

Communists extend their influence from North Vietnam and the northern provinces of Laos across the Plain of Jars into the capital, Vietiane. The Western world soon woke up to the idea that — in the words of the leader writers — Laos was a dagger pointing down into the heart of Southeast Asia.

Until then Vientiane had been a sleepy little place, more like a village than a capital, containing houses of a few great families, Buddhist temples, small houses on stilts along the side of the River Mekong, and the homes of humble rice farmers.

A visitor to the place in 1958 had a poor choice of accommodation. There was the *Somboun Inthavong*, a big wooden building with dark rooms where, Michael Field recalls, they never changed the sheets and pillowcases between guests. Or, if this proved intolerable, the newcomer could move up the road to languish at the *Bungalou*, a hostel for colonial officers which had been allowed to deteriorate badly. For dining out, Field recalls, there were two cafes, known to western habitues as Dirty Dan's and Filthy Fanny's.

When the Communist threat developed and the Americans began an aid programme to Laos, the hotel situation rapidly improved. The *Bungalou* was modernized into the splendid *Settha Palace*, and in 1963 the spacious *Lan Xang* opened its doors — the first Laotian attempt at a hotel of international standard.

However for all foreign correspondents and most diplomats visiting Vientiane in those restless years, the centre of activity was the *Constellation*, a hideous concrete building towering three storeys high above the low roofs of Main Street. The hot showers were a mere trickle, the windows were cracked and the beds rock-hard but this did not prevent the journalist from staying there because it was in the *Constellation* bar that he would hear what news was brewing, met informants and diplomats — and got his money changed at reasonable rates, by the amiable proprietor, Maurice Cavalerie, who was to become a legend among newsmen in the Far East.

It was said that he was of mixed parentage and was a former officer in the Chinese Nationalist forces. Certainly he knew everyone in Vientiane and was connected with many deals. As Field says he had a unique gift of combining warm humanity with business sense, and he kept his hotel going, with good food and drink, even during the worst days of the fighting in the late 1960s. Because it stuck up so high above the Vientiane roof-line the *Constellation* was a natural target for gunners on both sides, left and right. James Wilde, the Time-Life correspondent, had just left his room on the second floor when a shell tore through one wall and out through another. The hotel's outside wall was scarred with shrapnel and machine-gun and rifle bullets. The water-tank on the roof

was holed. But somehow Cavalerie kept the place running. Only when Laos was finally lost to the Vietnamese communist forces did he pack up and leave.

The war spread like a choking peat-fire into Cambodia (Kampuchea) where in 1970 Prince Norodom Sihanouk was overthrown in his absence and a group of generals found themselves in confrontation with the Communists. Phnom Penh, the capital of Cambodia, was livelier than Vientiane but compared with Saigon it was quieter, smaller and its hotels more relaxing. Old folks there can still remember the time of the youthful André Malraux, when he came with his wife Clara, and was sentenced to three years prison for allegedly stealing sculpture from the temple at Bantai Srei near Angkor. While awaiting trial (the sentence was later suspended) they had stayed at the *Grand*, the centre of Phnom Penh social life. Journalists in 1970 then stayed at the *Monorom* or the *Royal*. Covering the fighting was a sickeningly straightforward business. You hired a car and drove down any main road out of the capital until you came to a battle or an ambush. At least a dozen correspondents and photographers were killed or captured or simply never heard of again. Among them was Sean Flynn, the son of the American film star Errol Flynn, and his friend Dana Stone.

Gradually Indochina has been opening up to the tourists again, for there is an urgent need of foreign exchange. Soon the aircraft may even be landing at remote Vientiane bringing visitors to the Plain of Jars and the temples of Luang Prabang. But it is very unlikely they will stay at the old *Constellation* or meet the obliging Cavalerie. He belongs to a world that has long since vanished.

Macau, the Portuguese-administered enclave across the Pearl River estuary from Hong Kong, is called the "City of the Name of God"; among its backstreets fine baroque churches dream in the heat. Macau also houses Asia's great gambling centre, the *Lisboa Hotel*, where games of chance draw thousands to the tables day and night, while outside loan sharks wait — for the losers.

Not everyone goes to Macau to gamble. Traditionally it has always been a place of peace and quiet, dreaming of its history in the China trade. People from Hong Kong, worn down by the strains and tensions of money-making would spend a few days there, enjoying the restaurants and the Portuguese wine, visiting the old fort and strolling in the narrow streets. Now raucous traffic noise and building developments have taken much of the quiet out of Macau, save for the odd secluded corner. One of these shelters the *Bela Vista Hotel*, small, old and dignifed, with a broad marble staircase and balconies giving views across the bay to the islands.

Since we first stayed in Macau more than twenty-five years ago bigger hotels of international standard have changed its skyline; the latest are the *Regency Hyatt* on Taipa Island

and the *Pusada de Sao Tiago* built on the foundations of an old fort at the entrance to the inner harbour. But we always returned to the *Bela Vista* because of its peaceful atmosphere and its memories. Here in the early 1960s refugees from China escaped in their rickety boats and told of the hardships of life across the border during the famous "Three Bad Years." Here we stayed when our twelve-year-old son staked his pocket-money at fantan and, coached by the girl croupiers, won alarmingly (though he lost it all the next night). From our room on the second floor we could see through the branches of a huge tree the patched sails of Macau junks returning with the night's catch. Of course things have changed. The rooms have air-conditioning. The hotel's cooking is good. Hot water is available twice a day.

Hotel Bungalow, Vinh Long.

The historian of Macau, Father Manuel Teixeira, says the hotel was founded towards the end of the last century by an English couple — Captain William Edward Clarke of the *Heungshan* and his wife Catherine — though they sold it after a few years. During this time the French authorities in Indochina were looking for a suitable place as a convalescent home for sick and wounded French troops although they already had a military hospital in Macau. However the French offer to buy the hotel was rejected because, it was said, the British were strongly against allowing the French to acquire any more property in the area.

So, too, were the Portuguese authorities interested in using the building as a hospital but it was never found practicable. Nevertheless the *Bela Vista* was put to a variety of uses — as a secondary school; as a hostel for British Government students learning Cantonese; and, during the Second World War, as a lodging for refugees during the Japanese Occupation. Immediately after the war it served as a club for British servicemen stationed in Hong Kong. Finally at the end of 1948 the Macau Government sold the building to three Chinese ladies — Mesdames Kwok Chi Chan, Chan Sok Fong and Ng Tong Ying — and from then onwards it was run as a hotel by Mr Marques Pinto, later to be succeeded by his capable son.

When Hong Kong began life as a British colony in 1841 it was a rough provisional trading port protected by a large garrison. Officials and army officers needed no hotel accommodation and tourists were virtually non-existent. Later came lodging houses for seamen and the Hong Kong Club was founded, where well-connected travellers might stay. But it was not until December, 1892, that the new *Hong Kong Hotel* officially opened — a fine building putting completely into the shade the few mediocre guesthouses which by then were offering bed and board. Its attractions included the lifts — the brochure called them "hydraulic ascending rooms of the latest and most approved type"; and reflecting the state of security in Hong Kong at the time — "night porters and watchmen who are continually on duty."

Local business leaders ran the new hotel company. A major shareholder was Sir Ellis Kadoorie, and it was during his years as chairman that the company developed into a prosperous Far East hotel chain. On New Year's Day 1920, their next hotel, Hong Kong's *Repulse Bay Hotel*, was opened. An entire older generation of Hong Kong people remembers its verandah-cum-dining area looking out to sea, the large rooms, and the regular dances in the evenings. It was a place for honeymoons and parties, and for spending a relaxing weekend away from the bustle of the centre. British troops held out there desperately during the Second World War against the Japanese invader, rolling grenades and returning machine-gun fire along the carpeted corridors.

After the uneasy nightmare of enemy occupation the *Repulse Bay Hotel* was revived and continued to hold its special place in Hong Kong's affections despite the downtown competition. But in the development boom of the early 1980s the company demolished the old place to make room for massive new residential blocks. The wail of disapproval from the local clients was loud and long. Eventually the verandah restaurant and the gardens in front were restored to their original state and the customers came back.

The great project of the 1920s was the *Peninsula.* The Hong Kong and Shanghai Hotels Ltd., as the company was by now calling itself, had several hotels on the China mainland as well as three in Hong Kong; but the *Peninsula* was to surpass them all despite the many problems that delayed its birth. The restless state of affairs in the mid-twenties, with Chiang Kai-shek battling the warlords and with anti-British strikes paralyzing Hong Kong meant a heavy slice off the profits and doubts about the future. Foundation work at the new hotel — which included the sinking of 600 piles into the soft earth — added to the difficulties.

Then just when everything looked plain sailing and interior decoration already started, more trouble in China brought additional regiments to Hong Kong, and they took over the hotel temporarily as billets. Clifton Triggs, the company's engineer, said later: "When they handed the hotel back to us we practically had to renovate it. All the baths had to be replaced. I think they kept their guns in them."

Finally on 11 December 1928, the *Peninsula* was opened. It was a grand occasion with all the Colony's leading socialites present and enormous crowds joining in the specially-arranged opening parties.

fort. Along the street outside trees bent double, and high in the air loose scaffolding drifted through the mass of roaring rain; but inside the bedroom peace reigned and a dignified old waiter arranged the tray of drinks unperturbed.

Now the company (renamed the Peninsula Group) has opened the new 740-room *Kowloon Hotel* just behind the *Peninsula*, in step with the feverish development changing the whole face of Hong Kong in recent years, turning former wasteland and streets of drab tenements into a land of glittering high-rise towers.

So many new skyscrapers have soared into the mists

Hong Kong harbour in 1927.

The hotel has been modernized since but it still retains much of its first appearance, with the decorated ceiling and glittering chandeliers of the great lobby. It survived the Second World War although the basement was flooded as a result of the bombing and became a breeding place for millions of fierce mosquitoes. A big clean-up operation soon put everything right and the *Peninsula* has flourished ever since. For a newsman staying there during a severe typhoon in 1957 it represented relaxed, protective com-

In front of the *Peninsula,* Hong Kong.

drifting down from the Peak, so many old landmarks vanished. Buildings are as impermanent as people. The famous *Hong Kong Hotel* closed its door forever in 1954 but by this time the Hong Kong Land Company had put up the *Gloucester Building* on the corner next door, and ran this as a hotel until it began to acquire a decidedly old-fashioned look. Then the company went ahead with demolishing the old Queen's Building in central Hong Kong and replaced it with a luxury hotel — the famous *Mandarin*. It opened its doors in 1963 and achieved a world reputation it has maintained ever since.

Grand building, ornate facades, splendid entrance halls — all these have contributed towards making the latest Southeast Asian hotels a collection of high-rise dream palaces. The visitors come in groups, in package tours, by the score. There are so many temples to see, so many beauty spots, so many shops full of gems, silks, gold and silverware, porcelain and ivory. It is hard to recall a time when a city like Bangkok had only three hotels, among them the famous *Oriental*. The *Oriental* was always a place to head for, with the great Chao Phya flowing alongside and the open lawns reaching to the river's bank. The man behind the hotel's success was a Dane, H.N. Andersen who bought it in 1884, and in the following years he had it

Hong Kong Hotel at its beginnings, c. 1892.

rebuilt by Italian architects into a new, luxurious hostelry. On the day of reopening the management announced that everyone would be welcome from four o'clock onwards "when the fountains of magnanimity will be turned on and rain hospitality all around." Andersen went on to found the great East Asiatic Company and lived to a ripe old age of 85, in an era when tropical disease took a heavy toll of Westerners.

In 1892 the hotel is said to have been bought by Louis T. Leonowens, son of the celebrated Anna whose memoirs (which the Thais say are largely untrue) were the theme of the musical *The King and I*. Later the *Oriental* became the chosen staging post of writers and foreign correspondents, including Maugham, who had contracted malaria and nearly died. Noel Coward wrote: "There is a terrace overlooking the swift river where we have drinks every evening ... watching the tiny steam-tugs hauling rows of barges up the river against the tide. It's a lovely place ..."

A correspondent and his family on their first visit to Bangkok back in 1960 were booked by friends into a hotel not far from the *Oriental*, around the corner in Sathorn Road. This was the *Trocadero* where the assistant-manageress was a charming English girl who had come out East to marry a Thai prince; but something had gone wrong with the engagement and she would later be returning to Britain. But her kindness to a newly arrived family and the amiability of the Thai staff would always be

The old *Oriental*, Bangkok, 1922.

71

linked in the correspondent's mind with the *Trocadero*, with which he was to become a faithful client. Although his loyalty was somewhat tested during a long period of renovation when whole wall were knocked down, bedrooms invaded by dusts and the whole place abounded in mosquitoes. But he stood by the *Trocadero* and always stayed there when he passed through Bangkok.

Finally came the day when he arrived to find everything in shining order and the staff wearing colourful new uniforms. There was even a fine swimming pool. "But we are so very sorry," they said. "The hotel has been taken over for American R. and R. [rest and recreation for troops on short leave from Vietnam], so now you cannot stay here." He changed to the *Oriental* and did not return.

Throughout Southeast Asia the hotel business is fast expanding and hardly a month goes by without one of the international chains opening a grand new palace in some city boulevard. It is invariably well-managed and comfortable, and relying largely on the tourist's money. Staying at one of these places, eating one's way through the menu, relaxing in the pool, enjoying express laundry service and TV by the bedside — surely this is the essence of the sweet life. And you can have it in almost every city of the world. But here and there survive relics of other days, with a specialized appeal for customers who have been around in the area a very long time. The very facades of these hotels are a silent reminder of greetings and recognition, reviving professional memories of triumphs and setbacks, and friendships long cherished. To these places the traveller returns who is looking for the smile on familiar faces, the same room with the same view across the village roofs. After the years of caresses and hard knocks of work in Asia, staying at one of these favourite hotels is for him a kind of reassurance, a renewal of the mind.

On right
Leaving for the Orient.

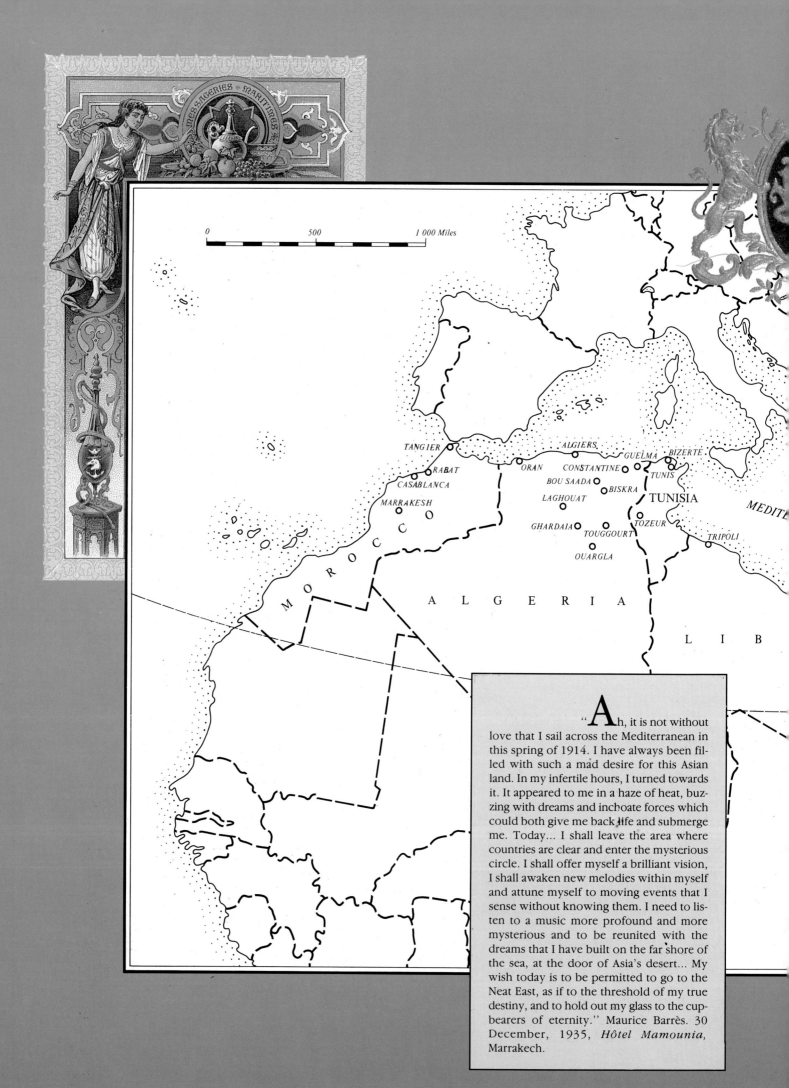

TANGIER
RABAT
CASABLANCA
MARRAKESH
M O R O C C O

ALGIERS
ORAN
CONSTANTINE
BOU SAADA
LAGHOUAT
GHARDAIA
TOUGGOURT
OUARGLA
GUELMA
BIZERTE
TUNIS
TOZEUR
TUNISIA
TRIPOLI
BISKRA

A L G E R I A

L I B

MEDITE

0   500   1 000 Miles

"Ah, it is not without love that I sail across the Mediterranean in this spring of 1914. I have always been filled with such a mad desire for this Asian land. In my infertile hours, I turned towards it. It appeared to me in a haze of heat, buzzing with dreams and inchoate forces which could both give me back life and submerge me. Today... I shall leave the area where countries are clear and enter the mysterious circle. I shall offer myself a brilliant vision, I shall awaken new melodies within myself and attune myself to moving events that I sense without knowing them. I need to listen to a music more profound and more mysterious and to be reunited with the dreams that I have built on the far shore of the sea, at the door of Asia's desert... My wish today is to be permitted to go to the Neat East, as if to the threshold of my true destiny, and to hold out my glass to the cup-bearers of eternity." Maurice Barrès. 30 December, 1935, *Hôtel Mamounia*, Marrakech.

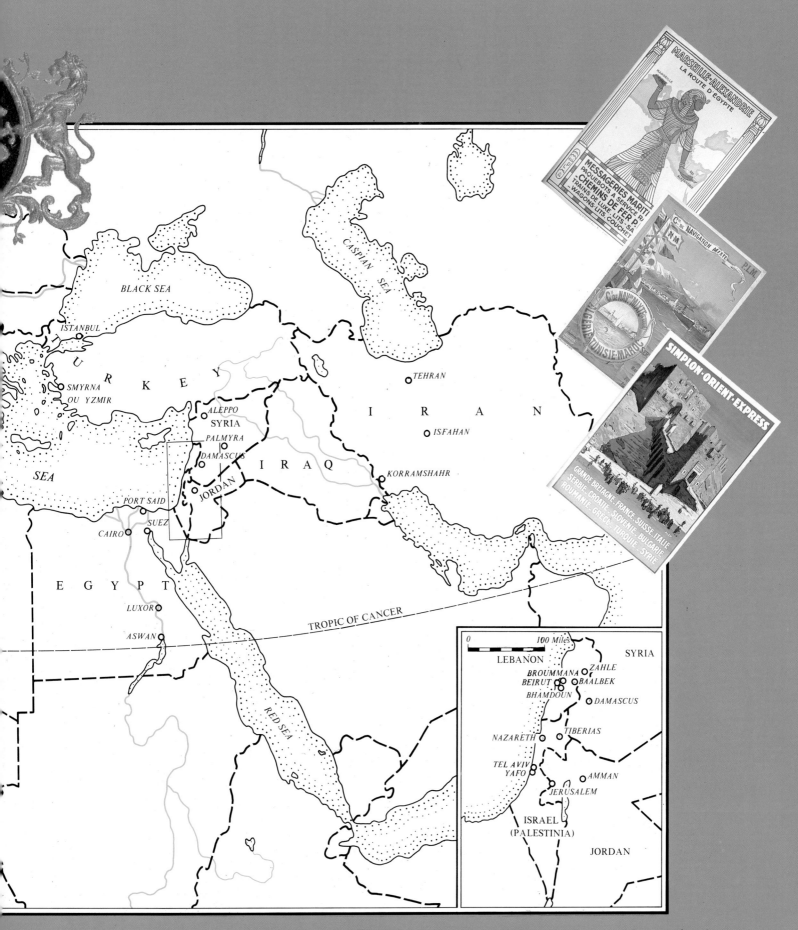

MARSEILLE-ALEXANDRIE
LA ROUTE D'EGYPTE

MESSAGERIES MARITI
PAQUEBOTS A SERVICE R
CHEMINS DE FER P.
TRAINS DE LUXE. LITS. SA
WAGONS-LITS. COUCHET

C⁰ DE NAVIGATION MIXTE
N M
P.L.M.
ALGERIE-TUNISIE-MAROC

SIMPLON-ORIENT-EXPRESS

GRANDE-BRETAGNE. FRANCE. SUISSE. ITALIE
SERBIE. CROATIE. SLOVENIE. BULGARIE
ROUMANIE. GRECE. TURQUIE. SYRIE

BLACK SEA

CASPIAN SEA

ISTANBUL

TURKEY

SMYRNA
OU YZMIR

TEHRAN

ALEPPO
SYRIA
PALMYRA
DAMASCUS

IRAN

ISFAHAN

SEA

IRAQ

JORDAN

PORT SAID

KORRAMSHAHR

SUEZ

CAIRO

EGYPT

LUXOR

TROPIC OF CANCER

ASWAN

RED SEA

0   100 Miles

SYRIA

LEBANON

ZAHLE

BROUMMANA
BEIRUT
BHAMDOUN

BAALBEK

DAMASCUS

NAZARETH

TIBERIAS

TEL AVIV
YAFO

AMMAN

JERUSALEM

ISRAEL
(PALESTINIA)

JORDAN

From Marrakech to Istanbul

M y darling Clemmie, This is a wonderful place, and the hotel one of the best I have ever used. I have an excellent bedroom and bathroom, with a large balcony twelve foot deep, looking out on a truly remarkable panorama over the tops of orange trees and olives, and the houses and ramparts of the native Marrakech, and like a great wall to the westward the snowclad range of the Atlas mountains...I am painting a picture from the balcony...How I wish you were here. The air is cool and fresh for we are fifteen hundred feet high, yet the sun is warm and the light brilliant.'' An extract from a letter from Sir Winston Churchill to his wife Clementine. Sir Winston was one of the *Mamounia's* most frequent guests. He would sometimes arrive without warning and move in with a paraphernelia of easels, canvasses, cases of whisky and such other things as were necessary for his comfort. The whole hotel would bubble over with excitement, and the porter whose duty it was to send off the great man's dispatches was ready to jump on his bicycle at any time of the day or night.

One evening in January 1943, at the end of the Casablanca Conference, two mud-splattered individuals appeared at the door of the hotel. They were Sir Winston with President Roosevelt, whom he had persuaded to spend twenty-four hours at the *Mamounia*; the journey had been long, the road bad and a breakdown had forced them to stop in the rain to change a wheel. Later, many of the important people who had to go to Casablanca or Rabat for political meetings sought to forget the cares of office in the *Mamounia*.

Above : the ''pavilion'' in the garden. This photograph was taken before the unfortunate restoration which took place in 1986. Right : Churchill at his easel in the garden of the *Mamounia*.

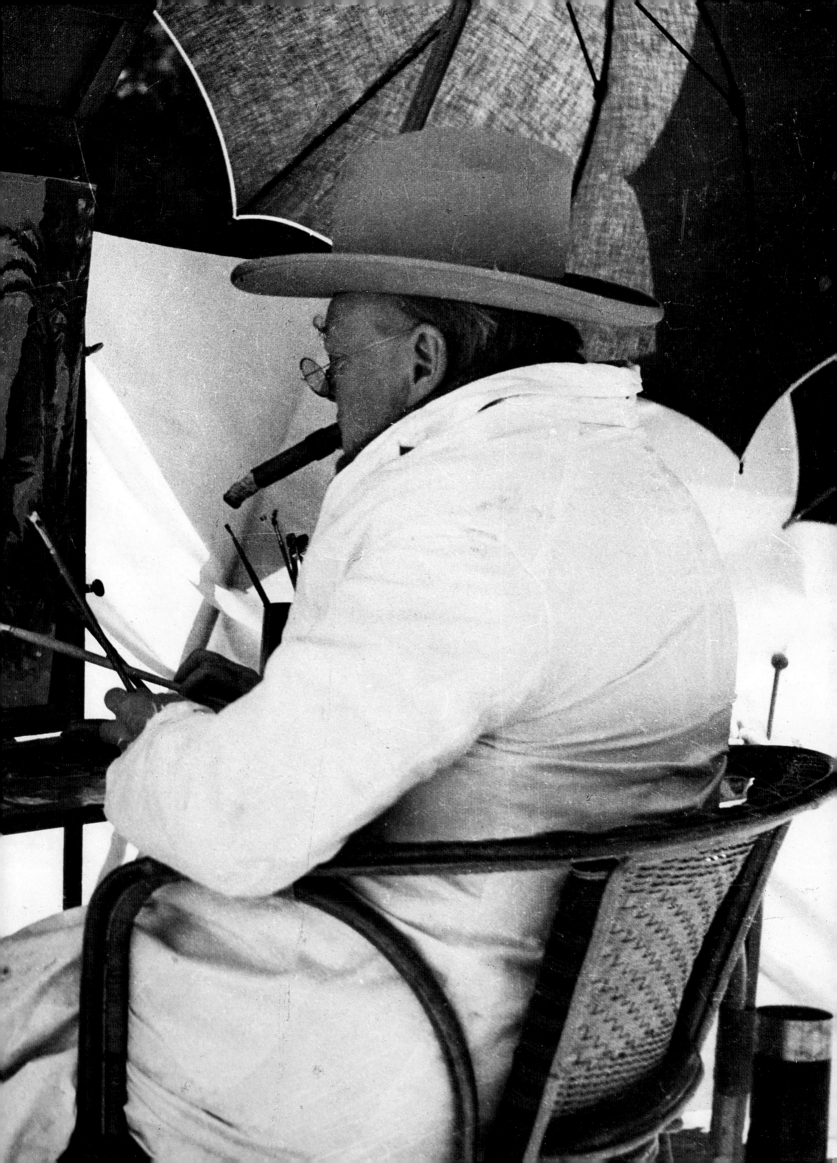

I n the 18th century, the four sons of Sidi Muhammad and the famous Lalla Fatima of Marrakech were each given a garden as a wedding present. These were fabulous, designed with great art, full of shaded, secret places and murmuring
fountains to which a complex network of underground pipes - the *khettaras* - brought the fertilizing waters of the Atlas.
When, in the early twenties, the Compagnie Générale Transatlantique and the Moroccan Railways decided to build a
grand hotel in Marrakech, one of these gardens was still in existence, that of the young sultan El Mamoun. Situated in the
shadow of the city walls and planted with olive trees it provided an ideal site. The hotel was built and, under the name of
the *Mamounia,* enjoyed a great reputation due particularly to its garden, even if certain guests failed to appreciate its rus-
tic charm : Rita Hayworth feared the effect of the Moroccan wind on her rich red hair which she had to wash every day; another guest is reported to have complained to the management that he was disturbed by the singing of the birds.
<u>Above</u> : A fountain in the garden; the ground is covered with small elongated pieces of baked clay, glazed on the outside
and set in the soil, a traditional techinque called *bejmat*. <u>Below</u> : lounges near what was until 1986 the main entrance .
This photograph was taken around 1950. <u>On the left page</u> : breakfast on the balcony of one of the bedrooms - a glimpse of
the thirties.

★ ★ ★ ★
grand hôtel

وزارة السياحة
مركز التكوين المهني للفنادق
الفندق الكبير
لو هران

Oran. Hôtel Continental, Façade latérale

The grand hotels of Oran and Algiers were monuments to the glory of French imperialism. They were designed to fit into towns planned on European lines, and were largely modelled on French patterns. Until the forties they catered to the provincial habits of the upper brackets of a colonial society. All this changed in 1942 with the landing of the Allied troops. Mixed and rather rowdy crowds descended on them. In the lounges of Algiers' *Aletti,* Josephine Baker, dressed in a tight-fitting dark blue uniform, was the star. Such popular figures as Jean Gabin and Jean-Pierre Aumont - also both in uniform - were to be found there, along with German spies and American intelligence agents posing as businessmen. <u>Above</u> : Algiers' *Hôtel Terminus et de l'Europe* around 1900. It later became the *Hôtel de l'Oasis*. <u>Below</u> : baggage label from the *Hôtel Aletti*. <u>On the left</u> page : the *Hôtel Albert Ier* in Algiers. Notepaper provided in the old days by the *Grand Hôtel* in Oran; the *Hôtel Métropole* and *Hôtel Continental* in Oran at the beginning of the century.

M ustapha supérieur, which occupies the side of one of the hills surrounding Algiers, was renowned as a pleasant residential area as early as the 19th century. It owes its name to the beautiful ''Villa Mustapha Pasha'' where the Dey held his court. In the 1897 issue of ''Where to Stay'', a fashionable guide to international grand hotels, the *Hôtel Continental et d'Orient* and the *Hôtel Kirsh,* the first luxury hotels built there, are praised for the beauty of the setting and the quality of their service. The *Saint-George*, probably Algiers' most beautiful hotel, was also built there on the site of a private mansion. Planned and decorated in the local style, it was outstandingly picturesque. In the fifties, the architect Pouillon enlarged and renovated it. Later named the *El Djazair,* it has lost much of its lustre although the charm of its terraced garden overlooking the Bay of Algiers remains intact.

<u>Above</u> : the *Hôtel Saint-George,* seen from the South around 1930. <u>Below</u> : baggage label. <u>On the right page</u> : terrace and lounge of the *Saint-George* in 1930.

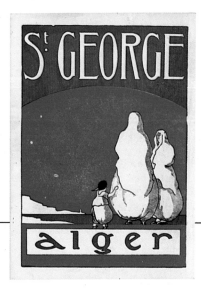

For the first early settlers and the self-important minor government officials, the grand hotel of Tunis and Algiers was a refuge where the proprieties of the mother country were maintained. But for subsequent generations they brought emancipation by encouraging the latest Paris chic : "In Tunis the young girls were the first to wear the short skirts promoted by Gabrielle Chanel, to get rid of their corsets... to accept a cigarette offered by their escorts, to cut their hair... They didn't care what people might say and actually dared to dance several times with the same partner, even in the tearooms of hotels like the *Tunisia Palace,* the *Majestic* or the *Royal.*" Nine Moati, 1983.

Above : the *Majestic,* Tunis, 1960s. Below : banquet of the Geographical Society at the *Tunisia Palace.* On the right page : lounges of the *Majestic* and baggage labels of the 1930s. Preceding pages : the *Grand Hôtel Bellevue* at Tozeur around 1900; one of the numerous establishments built in northern Africa by the Compagnie Transatlantique to cater for the more adventurous traveller; inset : P.L.M. advertisement.

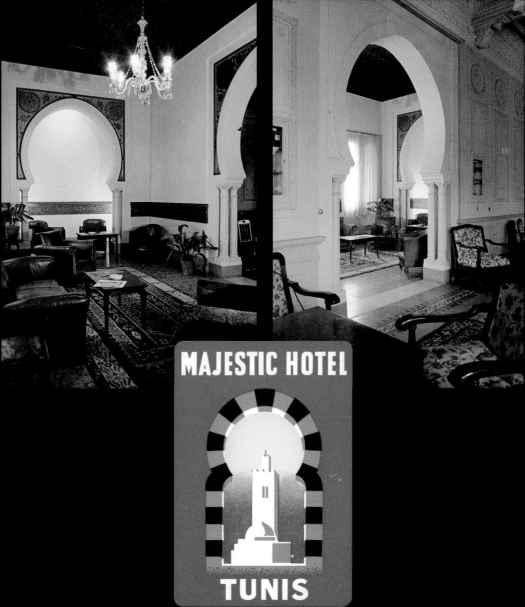

On the fifth day (the voyage out from Marseilles), the sea clouded by the silt from the Nile indicates the proximity of Egypt even if its low coastline cannot be differentiated from the rim of the horizon. Near Damietta, clumps of palm trees relieve the monotony of the scene, then the lighthouse of Port Said appears; one can see the houses on the beach and the statue of Ferdinand de Lesseps on the pier." *Guide to the Orient*, Madrolle, 1930.

Port Said and Suez were never places where people stayed for pleasure but rather necessary stops on the route of the great steamships. The hotels there were purely utilitarian and devoid of attraction. Even after the Suez Canal was built, they were only frequented by people in transit. They offered no more than rudimentary comfort but the absence of any competition allowed them to describe themselves as "Grand Hotels".

<u>Right</u> : the *Grand Hôtel Continental*, Port Said, around 1880.
<u>Above</u> : the *Grand Hôtel de Suez*, Suez, and the *Hôtel du Louvre et de France*, Port Said, around 1880.

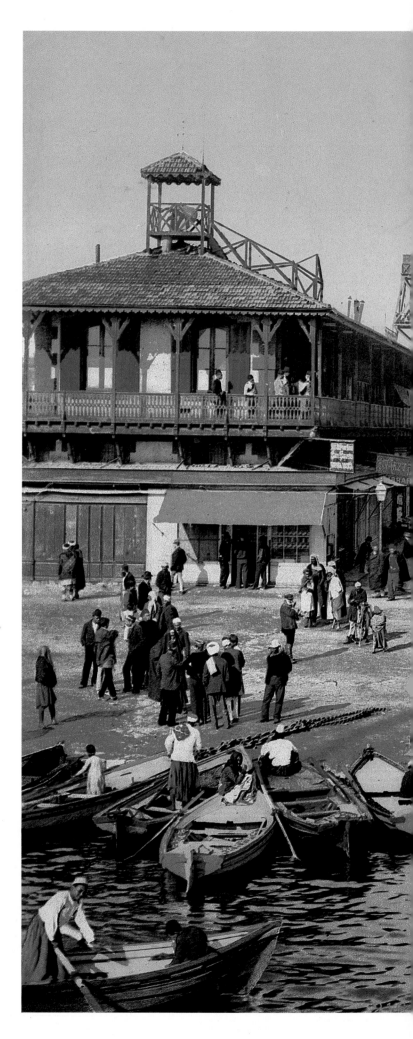

B uilt in 1865 on the luxuriant island of Gezira, the palace of the Khedive Ismail Pasha became one of the world's most famous hotels by the end of the 19th century. Designed to accommodate European VIPs invited for the inauguration of the Suez Canal, it had from the beginning all the features of a luxury hotel. In a theatrically oriental decor, the suite reserved for the Empress Eugénie was an exact replica of her apartments in the Tuileries. The great oriental hotels aimed to make the guest feel that he was simultaneously ''at home'' and in exotic surroundings.

<u>Above</u> : interior of the hotel, renamed the *Cairo Marriott* in 1982, after restoration and the addition of two towers. <u>Below</u> : the facade of the palace as it looked circa 1870. <u>On the left page</u> : the grand staircase of the *Gezira Palace Hotel* around 1900.

I n 1894, the Compagnie Internationale des Wagons-Lits (CIWL) set up a sister company, the Compagnie Internationale des Grands Hôtels. This was the first experiment of its kind. In the same year, the company acquired the palace of the Khedive at Gezira, and had it furnished by Maple & Co., the same firm which fitted out the famous luxury trains. However Cairo already had a beautiful hotel in *Shepheard's,* which had been established forty years before and which was virtually monopolized by Cooks'. The CIWL gradually gained ground on its great rival. The first step was to lure away Luigi Steinscheider, the highly competent manager of *Shepheard's,* and entrust him with the management of the *Gezira Palace.* The next move consisted of a barrage of publicity : several thousand pounds were given by Nagelmackers, the head of the CIWL, to encourage the Comité des Fêtes of Cairo to organize a grand gala which took place in 1896 at the Gezira : Rameses I was portrayed entering Thebes surrounded by musicians, camels and Egyptian soldiers in the costumes of the time of the pharaohs. In the end, the CIWL bought *Shepheard's,* and Cooks' clients had to rely on the rival company for their accommodation. CIWL's venture into the hotel trade was, however, shortlived : it ended in 1914.

<u>Above</u> : the inauguration of the Suez Canal, a mural in the *Cairo Marriott Hotel.* <u>Below</u> : poster advertising the Rameses gala at the *Gezira* and the Wagons-Lits company. <u>Page on the right</u> : lounges of the *Gezira Palace* around 1900. <u>Following pages</u> : the *Gezira Palace* around 1880.

24 Le Caire, Gezireh Palace Hotel, Léon Fogan

U nder the shade of the great awning of *Shepheard's,* the conscientious tourists quench their thirst, flasks and binoculars set aside, happy to have got through Sakkarah or Giza in the course of the morning. Inside, the lounge is in the old Cairo style with mosque lamps, fretted screens, low couches, shady corners behind *karamanieh portieres,* cathedral stained glass, and the pervasive seraglio scent of incense sticks.'' Paul Morand, 1936.
Above : the terrace of *Shepheard's* around 1900. Below : picture postcard, 1900. Left page : Cooks' sign on the facade of *Shepheard's.* It was here that the famous travel agent set up his first Cairo office. Following pages : right, the gardens around 1930; left, Anna Pavlova and Capt. Kruse at *Shepheard's* in 1923.

The extensive rebuilding of Cairo which begun under King Ismail continued until the first years of the 20th century. As Egypt's external debt grew and the British imposed their rule, villas and palaces went up in the European quarters of Gezira and Ezbekieh. Heliopolis, a satellite city built by Baron Empain's Belgian firm, rose from the desert with the *Palace Hotel* as its focus.

Flashy jet-setters, American beauties and the well-to-do came to winter in Cairo. Those who had long loved the city were horrified : ''What is all this ? What have we come to ? You would think you were in Nice or on the Riviera, or Interlaken, or any one of those exuberant cities where bad taste comes from the whole world to frolic during what are supposed to be the elegant months.... Everywhere blinding electricity; monstrous hotels showing off the false luxury of their would-be alluring facades; along the streets everything is fake, coats of whitewash over clay walls; a jumble of styles, the rococo, the romanesque, the gothic, *art nouveau,* the pharaonic and, above all, the pretentious and ludicrous.'' Pierre Loti, 1908. <u>Above</u> : facade of the *Palace Hotel* of Heliopolis around 1920. <u>On the left page</u> : the same hotel seen from the terrace of a private apartment.

A bove : group of tourists having their picture taken in the gardens of the Heliopolis *Palace Hotel* around 1920.
Below : picture postcard, 1900. On the right page : main lounge of the *Palace Hotel* in Heliopolis in 1920.

Facade of the Cairo *Hôtel Continental*, photographed by Bonfils around 1880. This hotel, which still exists under the name of the *Continental-Savoy*, was situated not far from the Opera House - burnt down in 1971 - and opposite the *Ezbekieh Hotel*. It was next to *Shepheard's* but there was no rivalry between the two, *Shepheard's* being the exclusive haunt of the British, and the *Continental* the traditional meeting place of the French.
On the left page : gardens of the *Hôtel du Nil*, in the heart of Cairo, on the Corniche around 1900. On the following pages : on the terrace of the *Helouan Hotel*, visitors who have come to take the waters at Helouan. This charming spa which has today become the centre of a big industrial complex was fashionable for a time at the beginning of the century. The Khedive Tauwfid had much faith in its waters which are similar to those of Aix-les-Bains.

A fter an evening spent at the *Mena-House Hotel* where gypsies played their melancholy and dissonant melodies which seem to evoke every possible passion, I went to contemplate the Sphinx bathed in moonlight...It appeared to me more imposing, as if transfigured. The magic of the moon seemed to recreate its mutilated features... I came back to the terrace of the hotel. The air was getting cooler. The big awning vibrated in the east wind. I sat under it without being able to shake off the sublime emotion created by this place which resembles the temple of the Absolute or to escape the insidious charm of the bright night, of the heavenly air.'' Édouard Schuré, 1898.
Above : American tourists on the terrace of the Giza *Mena-House* around 1920. When in 1880, Mr and Mrs Head bought this ancient khedival palace they named it "Mena House" after a pharaoh who united Upper and Lower Egypt in a single empire. It was converted into a hotel ten years later. Below : baggage labels. On the left page : gardens of the *Louxor Hotel* at Luxor around 1900.

W hen, at the end of the 19th century, the traditional pilgrimage to the Holy Land was resumed, Jerusalem became a sort of oriental Lourdes and the city had to be equipped with all the facilities required by international tourists. As everywhere else, many hotels were built at that time but even the best of them only enjoyed a mediocre reputation. There was a single exception, the *Grand New Hotel* which was recommended by Cook. It was the only hotel with decent bathrooms.

It was only in the 1920s, when Jerusalem became the capital of Palestine, then under the British mandate, that the idea of building a large, modern hotel was considered. It was the Mosseris, an influential Jewish family in Egypt who already controlled *Shepheard's*, the *Continental* and the *Mena-House*, who set up the *King David* in Jerusalem in 1931.

Until 1948 the hotel remained closely linked with Egypt : the managers were sent from Cairo, the shareholders' meetings took place at *Shepheard's* and the staff was Egyptian : tall Sudanese bearers wearing baggy trousers and white gloves, young bellboys in dark green, gold-braided coats. The chefs were Italian but the food was sent daily from Cairo by train.

Above : the *King David's* porter. Left : the *King David* in the 1930s. Previous pages : the *Grand New Hotel* in Jerusalem, near the Jaffa gate. 1929.

T,ravelling to the Middle East became more and more fashionable after 1850. It led not only to extensive building activity in order to equip cities with the necessary facilities but to the creation of a new profession, that of "dragoman" (see p. 246). Travellers who arrived exhausted and ignorant of local customs were happy to be met on their arrival by someone on whom they could rely to advise them, map out their itineraries, and serve as guide and protector. Such people could talk entertainingly in many languages and were familiar with European ways. They could solve any problem that might confront tourists, organise excursions and recommend the best hotels (with whom they worked in close contact).

An Englishman, Elias Warburton, described one of them whom he met in 1858 while travelling from Beirut to the Holy Land : "a young Syrian Christian, very handsome and dandified in proportion, with a dress resembling that of the muleteer, only of more elegant fashion and gaudier colours; he carried a brace of pistols on the high pommel of his Turkish saddle, a formidable sabre by his side, and my gun slung over his shoulder." This dragoman was, in fact, a man by the name of Nicola Bassoul who, after becoming rich, set up one of the oldest and most famous hotels of Beirut, the *Grand Hotel d'Orient,* better known as the *Hôtel Bassoul.*

Above and left page : In the main lounge of the *Bassoul,* cast-iron stove and couches covered with handwoven material. Around 1980.

Chest of drawers inlaid with ivory and mother-of-pearl, with a marble top; piece of furniture signed and bearing the date 1892, *Hôtel Bassoul,* Beirut, around 1980. <u>On the right</u> : the main lounge, around 1980.

Until recently, Nicola Bassoul's heirs continued to live in one of the wings of the hotel. It is probably because of this that the building was not damaged, the furniture kept intact and a typically oriental way of life preserved. Among the night-clubs, bars and modern hotels of Beirut, the *Bassoul* remained unchanged until finally the civil war got the better of it. It was, as John Carswell - the photographer who took the pictures of the *Bassoul* shown here - testifies, "a friendly and cheerful place to stay, and the only hotel in my experience where, arriving late at night, the sleepy night watchman would greet one from his bed just inside the door and, gesturing to a row of keys, tell one to choose whatever room one liked."

Taxi! To the *Saint-Georges*. The driver looks at me, hesitates...Nobody goes to the *Saint-Georges* these days. Before, ah! before, it was the pride of the city! It was not the *Ritz* for sure but everyone that counted met there...You could see army officers with sword and white gloves, bankers, well known journalists, actors and musicians on their way to Baalbek, whores...of the building which was probably impossible to raze to the ground there remains only a square structure, bare and hollow...'' Jules Roy, 1984.

<u>Above</u> : the *Hôtel Saint-Georges,* Beirut, around 1940. <u>Below</u> : the *Bassoul* or *Hôtel d'Orient* and the *New Royal Hotel* (avenue des Français), Beirut. <u>On the right</u> <u>page</u> : the *Grand Hôtel* of Aïn Sofar, Mount Lebanon, around 1895. The great Lebanese Christian families contributed to the success of the Aïn Sofar and were among its first shareholders.

Hotel, village et gare d'Ain Sofar, Mont Liban

Bonfils

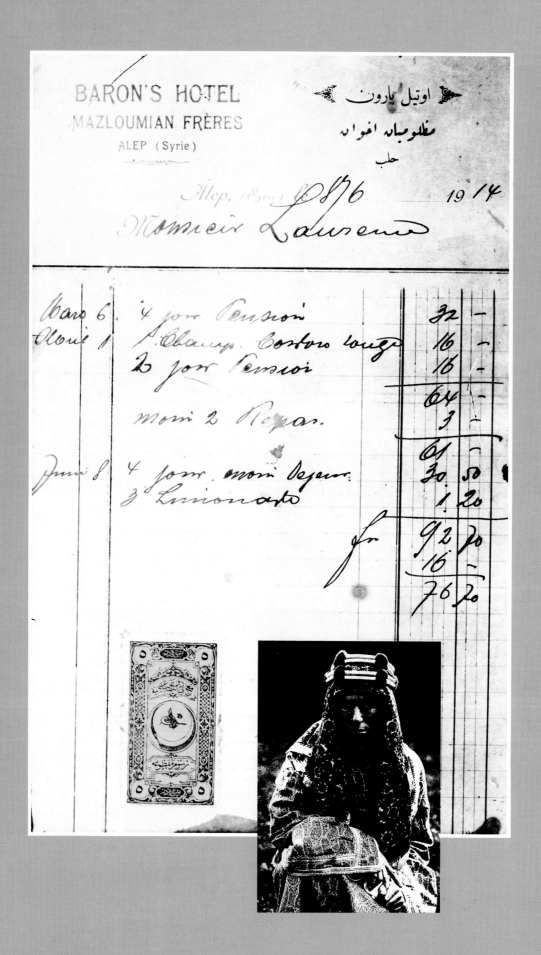

BARON'S HOTEL

MAZLOUMIAN FRÈRES

Oթեl Պարոն

ՄԱՉԼՈՒՄԵԱՆ ԵՂԲԱՐՔ

Հալեպ

اوتيل بارون

مظلومياه اخواد

حلب

Alep, (Syrie) *le* 19

A family of hotel keepers. the Mazloumians, founded *Baron's Hotel*. They came to Aleppo in the 1880s and set up the city's first hotel, an unpretentious, convenient place. Two Mazloumians of the next generation, Onnick and Armen decided in 1909 to build a new hotel - the *Baron's Hotel*. As its name indicates, it was intended to be luxurious. "Baron", however, is simply the Armenian word for "Mr", and the staff of the hotel always used it when they adressed the owners. Foreign guests were delighted to find themselves in such distinguished company.

At the time of its inauguration in 1911, the hotel was situated in the middle of a wood outside the town. Its guests could enjoy the peace of the countryside; and duck shooting from the windows of the *Baron's* bedrooms as one of their favourite pastimes. Aleppo has grown so much since those days that the *Baron* is now in the middle the city. It was nationalized in 1966 and Koko, the last of the Mazloumians, who no longer owns it but still manages it, is doing his best to save the building from demolition.

Above : first writing paper provided for the *Baron's* guests and a baggage label of the 1930s. On the left page : bill of Lawrence of Arabia when he stayed at the *Baron* in 1914. A bottle of Cordon Rouge had been included in his bill by mistake. As he only drank water, the item was deleted.

1911 stationary

David Rockefeller and Koko Mazloumian in 1970. Below : facade of the *Baron* in 1950. On the right page : 1 - arrival of the Duchess of Bedford, a regular guest at the *Baron* in the 1930s; 2 - the Swedish Royal Family in the 1930s; 3 - the Lindberghs once stayed briefly at the *Baron*; 4 - Amy Johnson and Jimmy Woods; 5 - Tito and Abdel Nasser making speeches from the terrace of the hotel; 6 - The *Baron* became a stopover in the 1930s for the Calcutta - Stockholm rally; 7 - military parade in front of the hotel in 1943.

On remarquera que la disposition de ce second hotel Toka... différente de l'autre qui lui fait v... l'autre est au bord de l'eau, même ... le Summer puis vers un magnifiqu...

HOTEL
MÉGUERDITCH TOKATLIAN
THERAPIA
HAUT BOSPHORE

L'un des hotels Tokatlian à Thérapia à l'entrée du petit golfe et en face du Summer Palace également tenu par Tokatlian.

The European shore of the Bosphorus, luxuriant, lined with terraced gardens, watered by limpid springs and rivers, was - as Castellan wrote in the 19th century - ''the meeting place of all the wealthy voluptuaries of every nation.'' In 1900, Therapia (or Tarabya), which stretches along a straight coastline at the foot of a great cliff, became a charming summer resort. As soon as the weather turned hot, Tokatlian's hotels were filled with tourists eager to escape the city and became for a few months the haunt of all those who usually stayed at Istanbul's *Pera Palace* which, in the beginning of the century, was also managed by Tokatlian.

T he *Pera Palace* was built in 1892 on a hill overlooking the Golden Horn in the Pera, a district of Istanbul, for passengers on the Orient Express. Ataturk was one of the most regular of its famous guests. In the suite which was always reserved for him and which has been left unaltered, the clocks show the exact time of his death. And it seems that, in the *Pera Palace,* time has stopped : no undue modernization has come to disturb the old fashioned pomp and the mild lack of comfort. The charm of the past has been preserved.

<u>Above</u> : military parade in front of the *Pera Palace* around 1918. <u>Below</u> : baggage label. <u>On the right page</u> : the dining room and the billiard room around 1895.

Abdullah frères

Salle à manger
Pera-Palace

Abdullah frères

Salle de billard
Pera-Palace

U. S. S. R.

TURKEY

IRAQ

IRAN

AFGHANISTAN

RAWALPINDI
LAHORE

SIMLA

BIKANER *DELHI*

PAKISTAN

UDAIPUR

JODHPUR *JAIPUR*

AGRA

GWALIOR

NEPAL

BHUTAN

KARACHI

BANGLA-DESH

CALCUTTA

INDIA

BOMBAY

SECUNDERABAD

BURM

RANGOON

MADRAS

SRI LANKA

KANDY

COLOMBO *NUWARA ELIYA*

MOUNT LAVINIA

GALLE

C H

MED

INDIAN   *OCEAN*

0   500   1 000 Miles

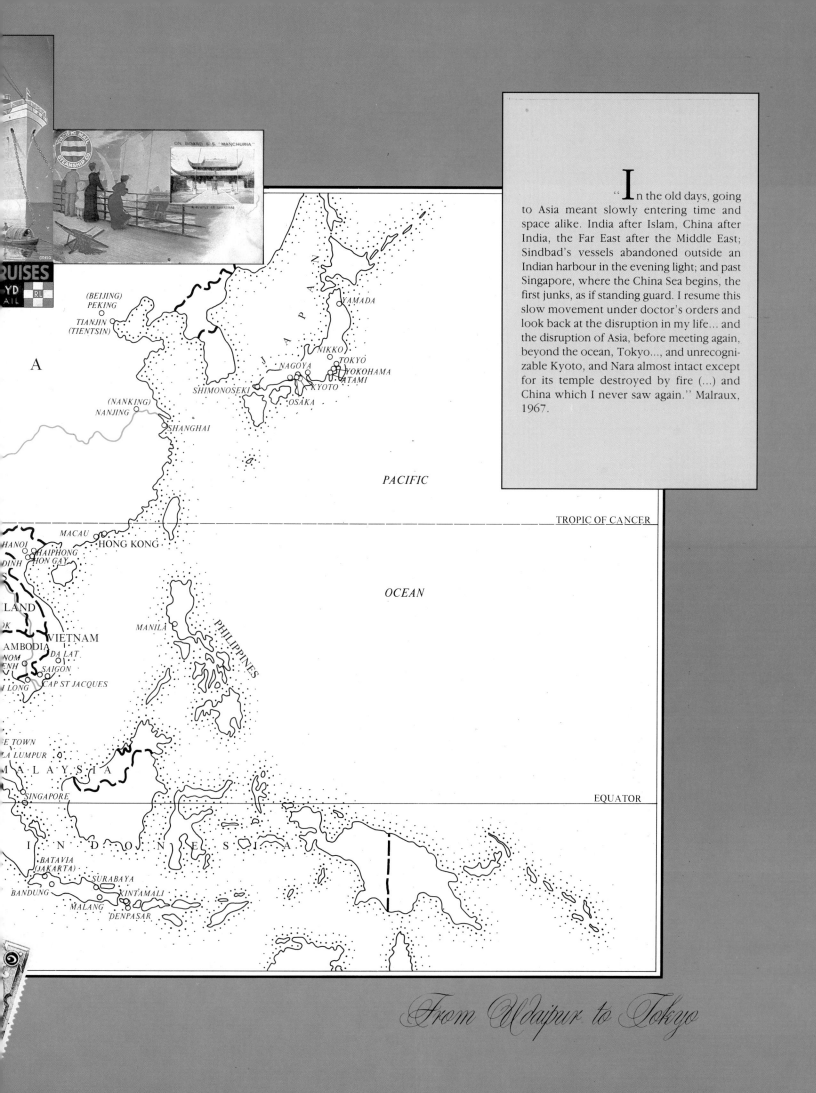

(BEIJING)
PEKING

TIANJIN
(TIENTSIN)

J A P A N

YAMADA

NIKKO
TOKYO
NAGOYA
YOKOHAMA
ATAMI
SHIMONOSEKI
KYOTO
OSAKA

(NANKING)
NANJING

SHANGHAI

PACIFIC

MACAU

HANOI
HAIPHONG
HON GAY
DINH

HONG KONG

OCEAN

LAND

VIETNAM
MANILA

PHILIPPINES

AMBODIA
DA LAT

NOM
ENH
SAIGON
LONG
CAP ST JACQUES

E TOWN
LA LUMPUR

M A L A Y S I A

SINGAPORE

TROPIC OF CANCER

EQUATOR

I N D O N E S I A

BATAVIA
(JAKARTA)
SURABAYA
BANDUNG
KINTAMALI
MALANG
DENPASAR

"In the old days, going to Asia meant slowly entering time and space alike. India after Islam, China after India, the Far East after the Middle East; Sindbad's vessels abandoned outside an Indian harbour in the evening light; and past Singapore, where the China Sea begins, the first junks, as if standing guard. I resume this slow movement under doctor's orders and look back at the disruption in my life... and the disruption of Asia, before meeting again, beyond the ocean, Tokyo..., and unrecognizable Kyoto, and Nara almost intact except for its temple destroyed by fire (...) and China which I never saw again." Malraux, 1967.

From Udaipur to Tokyo

T he *City Palace* of Udaipur in 1880. On the left, jutting out, is the Shiv Niwas, a wing added in 1860 and converted into a hotel in 1984 by the Taj chain. <u>Below</u> : hall of the *Shiv Niwas* in 1907. <u>Right page</u> : the same hall in 1986. It has been turned into a reception room for the hotel. <u>Previous pages</u> : the *Lake Palace*, Udaipur, around 1880. Built in 1746 as a guest house, in the 1960s it became the first princely palace to be converted into a hotel. <u>On the following pages</u> : another reception room of the *Shiv Niwas*, 1986.

I n 1923, for the third consecutive year, there was no rain during the monsoon in Rajasthan. To provide employment for his subjects and save them from starvation, the Maharajah Umaid Singh decided to build a new palace at Jodhpur - the Umaid Bhawan. Three thousand workers were employed on it and twelve miles of railway were built to transport blocks of sandstone from the quarry nearest to the hill on top of which the palace was to be built. Lanchester, a British architect who had helped Lutyens in planning the city of New Dehli, designed it. Work on the building lasted for almost two decades and it was only completed in 1942. It was a gigantic edifice. Originally there were three hundred and forty-seven rooms - of which eight were dining rooms - a banquet hall, a theatre, a ballrom and kitchens, both English-style and Indian; it was fully air-conditioned. In 1970, part of this palace, which already had the facilities available in the best international hotels, was transformed into a hotel. The Maharajah continues to live in the rest of the palace with his family.
Above : the present Maharajah of Jodhpur, 1986. Below : Christmas Eve 1943, meal organized at the *Umaid Bhawan* for R.A.F. personnel stationed at Jodhpur; on the menu, stuffed wild boar's head. On the right page : princely weddings at *Umaid Bhawan;* above, wedding of Maharajah Hanwant Singh, 1943 and, below, wedding of his sister, Princess Baijilal Rajindra Kumari, 1950; inset : family tree of the Rathors who had made Jodhpur the capital of their kingdom.

M ain entrance of the *Lalgarh Palace,* Bikaner, 1902. A wing of the palace was made into a hotel to which the name of *Lalgarh Palace Hotel* was given. Its architect, Samuel Swinton Jacob (1841-1917), drew his inspiration from the Rajput style to build this graceful monument of sandstone covered with fine sculpture. The old citadel of Bikaner was his model. Below : coming back from the hunt, around 1900. On the right page : billiard room decorated with hunting trophies and reception room, *Lalgarh Palace,* 1900. The rooms were laid out and furnished in a westernized fashion in deference to British guests. To this extent, the Prince may be said to have received his guests as the hotel managers of the time were accustomed to do.

A few days later I stopped at Jaipur, capital of Rajasthan, at the *Rambagh* which means "the garden of the God Rama." This was once the residence of the Maharajah, and the manager is one of his sons. He learnt the trade in a European hotel school and is most competent, but I cannot believe that this occupation will help him adapt to the life of a simple citizen." Vilold de Golish, 1973.

Above and on the right page : light and shade under the veranda, *Rambagh Palace,* 1987. This palace was built around 1840 during the reign of Maharajah Ram Singh II and was used as a hunting lodge. In the beginning of the 20th century, Maharajah Man Singh, who loved everything British, furnished the palace in western style and - an unheard-of luxury - provided a private polo ground adjoining it. The *Rambagh* became a residential palace in 1925 and was converted into a hotel at the beginning of the 1960s.

I t is almost midnight. The *Taj Mahal* is like a marketplace with the stalls pulling down their shutters. Inside the grand hotel, one of the most famous in the world, crisscrossed by the great tunnels of high ceilinged corridors and lounges (it is like wandering inside a gigantic musical instrument), only boys clad in white and porters in glamorous turbans can be seen, waiting hopefully for doubtful taxis...I persuade Moravia to...walk about near the hotel and take a few breaths of air of this first Indian night.'' Pier Paolo Pasolini, 1961.

<u>Above</u> : the facade of the *Taj Mahal* in 1935. <u>Below</u> : the back of the building where the main entrance should have been situated facing the sea if - so legend has it - the plan had not been misunderstood. Thanks to this mistake, most of the rooms look out on the ocean. This so disappointed the architect that he committed suicide. <u>On the left page</u> : galleries inside the *Taj*, 1986.

In British India, most of the big hotels were like enclaves enjoying exterritorial status. They were exclusively reserved for the British and other foreigners. No Indian was admitted except in rare cases and on the condition that native guests should not set foot in the lounges or dining rooms. This rule did not apply to the *Taj*. Tata, the famous industrialist who founded it, had been denied entry into one of Bombay's better known hotels. Understandably, he exempted the *Taj* from this prohibition. A luxurious decor and magnificent parties smoothed out the difficulties of cohabitation.
<u>Above</u> : reception given in the *Taj's* ballroom in 1920. <u>Below</u> : arrival of "Ataturk", a horse that waltzed and fox-trotted at a show organized in 1952. <u>On the left page</u> : above, seafront of the *Taj,* 1910; <u>below</u>, a military parade in the 1940s.

145

T he *Bycullah,* Bombay, 1871. Below : the *Oberoi Grand* (formerly *Grand Hotel*), Calcutta, 1987. On the right page : above, *Watson's Hotel,* Bombay, 1890 : below, the *Grand Hotel,* Calcutta, 1928 and the *Great Eastern,* Calcutta, 1918.

Rudyard Kipling stayed in the *Great Eastern* in the 1890s : "The *Great Eastern* hums with life through all its hundred rooms. Doors slam merrily, and all the nations of the earth run up and down the staircases. This alone is refreshing, because the passers bump you and ask you to stand aside...Fancy sitting down seventy strong to *table d'hôte* and with a deafening clatter of knives and forks! Fancy finding a real bar whence drinks may be obtained !" Rudyard Kipling, *From Sea to Sea,* 1899.

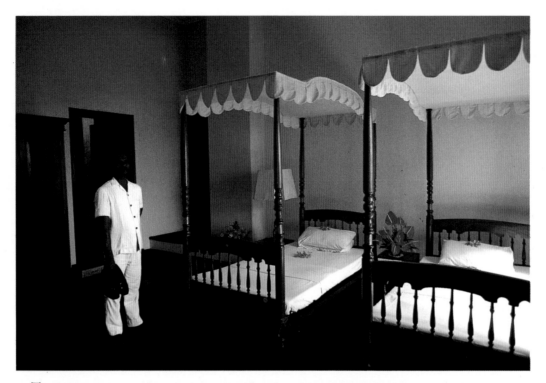

The *Galle Face Hotel* opened in 1864 in Colombo under the name of *Galle Face House*. It was only in 1984 that, after having been expanded and renovated, the building took on its present form. Superbly situated between the sea and the green grass of a race course, it was one of the most popular of the British Empire's fashionable resorts. Its preeminence was such that it was the first overseas hotel to be supplied with ''Pimms'', the drink favoured by the London gentry in the 19th century, which had not even reached the grand hotels of Cairo.

<u>Above</u> : a bedroom in the *Galle Face,* 1986. <u>Below</u> : picture postcard of the 1920s. <u>On the right page</u> : above, the seafront in the 1920s; <u>below</u>, entrance to the hotel around 1880. <u>On the previous pages</u> : the ballroom which served as both reception hall and dining room, 1986.

Billiard room of the *Hill Club*, Nuwara Eliya, 1986. Below : the *Hill Club's* coat of arms, designed in 1876 by a group of Scottish planters. It was only in 1930 that this building, originally the seat of a hunting club, became a regular hotel. From then on the presence of women was tolerated but, until 1940, they had to enter by the south door, with the luggage. On the left page : Lord Mountbatten's room, *Hôtel Suisse*, Kandy, 1986. This building, once the residence of a British Army officer, was bought in 1850 by a Swiss lady who transformed it into a guest house. On the following pages Mount Lavinia, residence of the British Governors, 1875. In 1877 it became the *Mount Lavinia Hotel*.

31 – Grand Oriental Hotel, Colombo.

The *Grand Oriental Hotel* (since renamed *Taprobane*), Colombo, around 1900. <u>Below</u> : baggage label of the *Queen's Hotel,* Kandy. <u>On the right</u> page : the *Queen's Hotel* during the festivities organized in 1897, on the occasion of Queen Victoria's jubilee; above, parade on the esplanade, with the hotel as a backdrop; <u>below</u>, the *Queen's* decked with flags; these ceremonies took place on 29 June, ''a bright day, with the old king smiling approval on these marks of loyalty to Queen Victoria... a sixty-gun salute was fired, the Lancashire troops presented arms, and the orchestra played the National Anthem.'' (*Ceylon Overland Observer*, 1 July, 1897).

S omerset Maugham's ''The Gentleman in the Parlour'' is set in 1922, in Bangkok's *Oriental Hotel*. Today his name has been given to a suite in the old wing of the hotel called the ''Authors' Wing''. Other suites - Conrad's - Graham Greene's and Noël Coward's - bear witness to the fact that in this hotel, all light and greenery, almost anything may happen, as Graham Greene has said, and you are likely to meet everyone.
<u>Above</u> : gardens of the *Oriental,* 1932. <u>Below</u> : Captain Andersen in 1903; he bought the old *Oriental,* founded in 1876, rebuilt it and opened it as a new and luxurious hotel in 1887. <u>On the left page, from top to bottom</u> : the *Oriental* as it was in 1887; it still exists, miraculously preserved under the name of the ''Author's Wing''; cocktail party in the open air, 1920; baggage label; entrance hall, 1947.

The *Raffles* was the pearl in the chain of hotels set up by the Sarkies, and their most thrilling undertaking. Yet, the whole thing started very badly for the two brothers, Tigran and Martin. The rent they had to pay for the recently opened *E & O* had just been doubled. ''A joke'', reported the Penang *Gazette,* ''which Mr Sarkies does not appear to appreciate, and he has consequently decided to seek new and, let us hope, happier hunting grounds.'' They then looked towards Singapore, prospering on the eve of Queen Victoria's jubilee, and decided to build a new hotel there. The only thing left to do was to find a name for it. Legend has it that Tigran, who was in charge of the negotiations, had a brainstorm. He rushed to the post office and wired his brother Martin in Penang a single word. The reply was equally short and contained the same word, magic and now legendary : *Raffles.*
Above : *Raffles'* menus and portrait of Arshak Sarkies who managed both *Raffles* and *E & O* until 1931. On the left page : *Raffles'* main entrance at the beginning of the century. Previous pages : *Raffles* which is today enclosed in an urban surrounding was originally a seaside hotel.

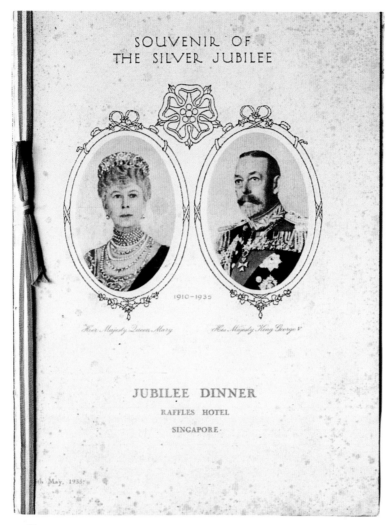

SOUVENIR OF
THE SILVER JUBILEE

1910-1935

Her Majesty Queen Mary   *His Majesty King George V*

JUBILEE DINNER

RAFFLES HOTEL

SINGAPORE

th May, 1935

For decades, if you wished to meet someone in Singapore, or even in Asia, the watchword was, "See you at *Raffles*", as time-honoured as the phrase, "See you at the *Savoy*." As early as 1890, the hotel's advertising, which in fact consisted of the appearance in the newspapers of endless lists of its fashionable guests, bore witness to its success. *Raffles*, as Maugham was to put it, became the melting-pot of "all the fables of the exotic East" - from a certain summer afternoon in 1921 when two gentleman captured the last of Singapore's tigers under the hotel's billiard table, to 15 February 1942 when the Japanese, entering a city in flames, found the elegant guests of *Raffles* dancing a last sad waltz. There is no longer any danger of finding a wild beast wandering in the corridors. and the sea which once lapped the edge of the gardens is no longer visible. In the sixties there was talk of demolishing the famous establishment but nothing was done and *Raffles* survives intact. The old rooms opening onto verandas have retained their seaside charm; at midday the Tiffin Room is still the most delightfully cool spot in Singapore. And at nightfall, when the lights come on in the Palm Court and the air is filled with the scent of flowers, you quite forget that the hotel is but an oasis surrounded by skyscrapers...

<u>Above</u> : gala menu for the celebrations in honour of Queen Mary's and King George V's Silver Jubilee held at *Raffles* in May 1936. <u>Right-hand</u> <u>page</u>: the copious breakfast menu in 1889. <u>Previous pages</u> : gallery leading to rooms giving on to the Palm Court. Following pages : three views of the floors overlooking the Tiffin Room, 1987.

T hree of Penang's large hotels around 1920 - the *Raffles-by-the-Sea* or *Bellevue Hotel*, former residence of a wealthy Chinese; the *Runnymede*, originally built for Sir Stamford Raffles then reconstructed and converted into a hotel around 1920; the *Springtide*, an elegant hotel by the sea. <u>On the left page</u> : above, the *Runnymede*, now occupied by the army, 1987; below, the *Raffles-by-the-Sea* transformed into a school, 1987. <u>On the previous pages</u> : the *Springtide*, 1987. The hotel was closed down and the ruined building is used as a meeting place by missionaries; in the large ballroom, its great windows broken, the sound of hymns and sermons have replaced the dance tunes once played by lively orch stras.

Penang's *Eastern and Oriental* really became a luxury hotel only after the arrival of Arshak Sarkies who took over the management from his elder brothers, Martin and Tigran. A contemporary journalist described him in the Penang *Echo* as a "haughty and somewhat arrogant man, a genuine Eastern aristocrat who was nonetheless liked by one and all, from the bare-footed Tamil elevator man to princes and millionaires." The whimsical nature of this curious character - often seen dancing alone on the polished floor of the ballroom, a glass of whisky balanced on top of his bald head - made for the success of the *E & O* but also spelled its ruin. In the twenties, at a time when the great Depression was in the forseeable future, Arshak, bent on achieving his dream, was spending money like water. Nothing was too good if it contributed to the fame of his hotel : there were endless magnificent receptions whose illuminations lit up the sea front to the accompaniment of the furious rhythm of the fox-trot. The hotel also suffered from the carefree way in which its regular guests - adventurers out of funds or ruined rubber planters - left without settling their accounts. Arshak was the most understanding of men and did not press them to pay. He was more interested in grandiose plans for the renovation of his hotel. In 1931, when he died, the *Eastern and Oriental* was bankrupt. It was bought shortly afterwards by its main rival, the *Runnymede*. This marked the end of a period of which the *E & O* is a nostalgic reminder.

Above : 1 - The ballroom, inaugurated in 1923. 2 - The dining room in the 1920s; 3 - The main building facing the sea in the 1920s; 4 - The Victory wing, built in 1922. On the left page : street facade, 1986.

RAFFLES HOTEL

BILL OF FARE

BREAKFAST

Singapore *2ⁿᵈ June* 189*5*

1   Porridge

2   Fried Fish

3   Mutton Chops

4   Devilled Fowl

5   Cold Beef & Salad

6   Boiled Eggs

7   Cheese

8   Fruit

9   Jam

10   Tea or Coffee

NOTE. – Hotel Boys with Numbers.

N. B. — Kindly send written orders for Wi...

After meals take a ...

I n the 19th century, the small mound on which the *Goodwood Park Hotel* was built was the property of William Scott, a first cousin of Sir Walter Scott. All along what is now Scott Road stretched a plantation of nutmeg trees infested by tigers coming from the South of the peninsula, which caused much fear and sometimes death. In 1890, William Scott was ruined by the disease which wiped out all the nutmeg trees of the island and had to sell his estate. Part of it was bought by the German community in Singapore to build a club which was named the Teutonia Club. The elegant building meant to house it was inaugurated on 21 September 1900 and is now the old wing of the *Goodwood Park Hotel*. Before it became one of Singapore's most famous hotels, the Teutonia Club was successively declared ''enemy property'' during the First World War, used as a powerhouse for three years and converted, in 1921, into a restaurant and entertainment hall known as Goodwood Hall. In 1922 it became Singapore's first cinema and on 14 December of the same year Anna Pavlova appeared there in a performance of *Swan Lake*. It opened as the *Goodwood Park Hotel* in April 1929.

Above : the staff - all men except for the stewardess - in front of the entrance of the hotel in 1949. On the right page : details of the architecture of the old wing, restored in 1980.

On the previous pages, the *Brastagi Hotel,* Brastagi, in the 1930s. ''The hotel (in Brastagi) could not be better. It is ideally situated. Behind, as a backdrop, is the sulphur breathing crater of the Sibajak, and in front the eyes rest on the green fields of the Karo plateau. It is an astonishingly lovely place.'' W.R. Foran, 1936.

One branch of the Sarkies family settled in Indonesia. John Martin Sarkies opened the *Sarkies Hotel* in Surabaya and, in the same city, Eugène-Lucas Sarkies set up the *Oranje Hotel* in 1910. Thirty five years later it passed into Indonesian history. On 19 September 1945, an angry crowd stormed into the hotel; the Dutch flag was hauled down from the roof and replaced by the Indonesian red-and-white emblem while the spectators cheered wildly.

Inset, left : John Martin Sarkies and his family around 1900. Facing page : wedding of one of Sarkies' sons at Sarkies Hotel around 1920. Right : the villa of the Sarkies in Surabaya in 1920.

181

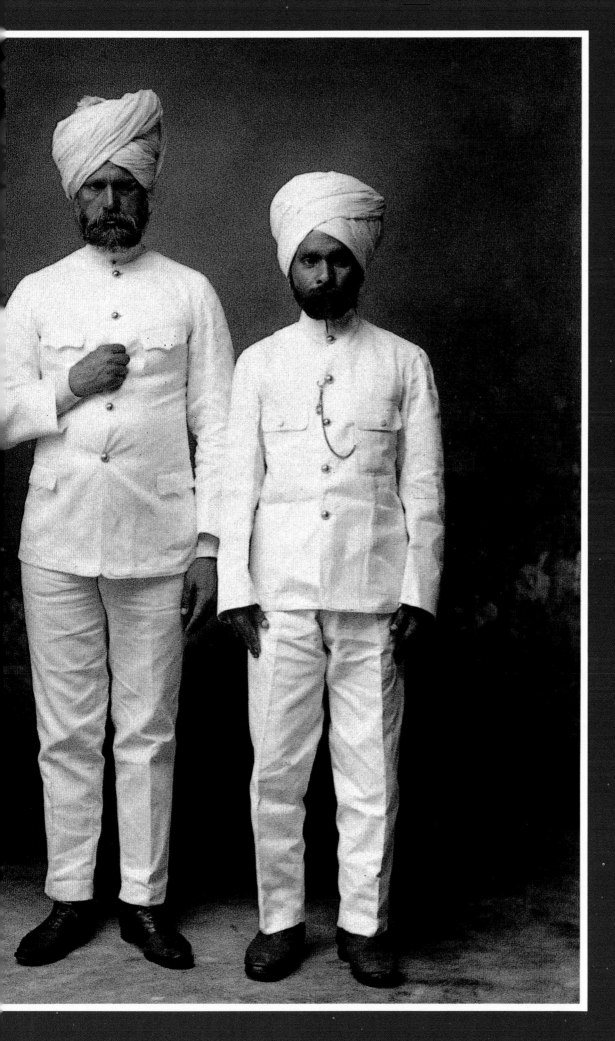

"The *Hôtel des Indes* where I stayed is famous in the Far East and it deserves to be. It is built on very extensive grounds - 16 acres, to be precise - and is surrounded with magnificent trees. At the entrance to the main building are two Waringin (banana trees). I have made some brave but unsuccessful attempts to get acquainted with the *rystafel*. Yet the *Indes* is famous for its *rystafel*. It is brought in by twenty-four Javanese waiters walking in single file, each holding two dishes over his head. The procession stretches from the kitchen to the dining room like a gigantic caterpillar. To amuse myself I counted how long the whole procedure took - exactly 15 minutes." W.R. Foran, 1936.

1 - Main entrance of *Hôtel des Indes* seen from the canal, 1903. 2 - Hotel buggies waiting in front of the main building, 1903. 3 - The reception hall in 1906. 4 - Mr Gantvoort checking the accounts in one of the lounges. He took over the management in 1906. 5 - Some members of the staff in 1907. At that time the hotel had a staff of 155, 15 of them being Europeans, including 3 cooks. 6 - When Gantvoort took over, most rooms were modernized and bathrooms were added to them. Every two rooms enjoyed the exclusive services of one bearer. 7 - The dining room in 1906; renovated in 1913. 8 - A private dining room, 1906. 9 - Veranda in front of a bungalow, 1906. The bungalows were built on either side of the main building to which they were linked by covered galleries. 10-11-12 - Verandas, 1907.

T he *Grand Hotel Preanger* was established in Bandung at the end of the 19th century and renovated at the beginning of the 1930s by the architect C.P. Wolff Schoemaker who added an extra wing. In its modernized version, the *Preanger* was a remarkable example of how aesthetic and architectural experiments carried out in the Netherlands could be applied in Asia. The layout and decoration of the lounges showed the influence of the avant-garde Amsterdam School which sought to achieve an harmonious blend between the styles of Frank Lloyd Wright (American), German Expressionism and decors copied from various oriental sources. The *Preanger* exemplified this astonishing cultural synthesis.

Above : the hotel's main entrance, 1935. Below : cover of a publicity booklet, 1936. On the right page : facade of the building before renovation, around 1900; the veranda in 1935 and the main lounge. The wainscotting on the walls was of two different shades with dark blue panels in between; the hotel orchestra gave a daily concert here.

I naugurated on America's Independence day - 4 July, 1912 - the *Manila Hotel* was hailed by the Manila *Times* as ''a monument to Americanism.'' The design of the American architect Parsons was executed by a New Yorker working with an all-American team. In 1935 a suite with a terrace was set aside on the top floor for General MacArthur, then military adviser to the Philippine Government. He stayed there until the Japanese invasion. Four years later, when the Allied Forces reconquered Manila, an American lieutenant was told, as he remembers today, that the specific mission of his unit was to free the *Manila Hotel* : ''We were told that the Boss (MacArthur) wanted to get back his former apartment -intact.'' Unfortunately, the suite was destroyed by a fire. In his *Memoirs* MacArthur wrote : ''A smoking gun in his hand and a victorious smile on his face, the young lieutenant who was commanding the patrol shouted out to me : 'Everything is O.K., Boss.' But for me nothing was O.K. I felt bitter about this place that I had been so fond of.'' The hotel reopened in 1946. Above : the *Manila Hotel* entrance hall, 1986. Below : publicity material of the 1930s. On the right page : 1 and 2 - the barber shop and a room, 1912; 3 - reception given for the first Miss Universe, 1952; 4 - Richard Nixon, 1953; 5 -Eisenhower and Rocky Marciano, 1953; 6 - *Manila Hotel* after the battle of Manila; at the top of the tower, what is left of MacArthur's apartments, 1945; 7 - MacArthur embraces the hotel telephone operator; next to him Mrs MacArthur, 1961.

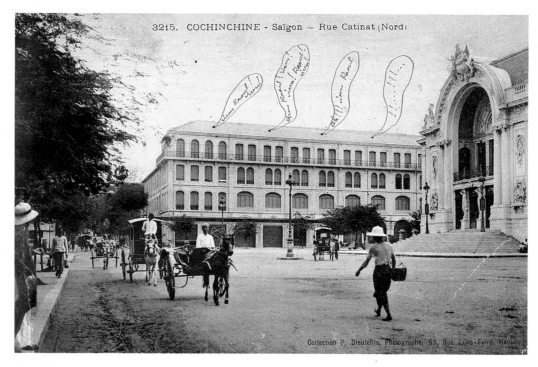

A t the *Continental Palace* the afternoons were devoted to the siesta or, as is suggested in this picture postcard, to other pleasures. "Sleepiness seems to overtake everyone. The Annamese *maîtres d'hôtel* alone are wide awake, these old and wrinkled servants who are part of the furniture. They move about...ethereal, like the mocking spirits of the place." Lucien Bodard.

Below : a room in the *Continental,* publicity material of the 1920s; Saigon at the end of the 19th century. On the right page : dining room and entrance of the *Grand Hôtel de la Rotonde* around 1930. Previous pages : the terrace of the same hotel in 1930.

2280

Letter from A. Messmer (contractor) to the secretary to the Governor-General of Indochina, dated 7 September 1931 : ''I think it my duty to state forcefully that the Government must do everything in its power to attract tourists, especially since Indochina is facing unprecedented difficulties. It must not hesitate to go through with its programme of hotel building. The Colonial Exhibition will, I think, be as successful as expected. It will result in a flow of tourists. They will bring money that the country needs. At the moment nothing is ready to provide them with decent facilities''.
Above : dining room of the *Langbian Palace* built in Dalat in 1915. Below : notepaper provided to the guests of the *Grand Hôtel d'Angkor et Hôtel des Ruines,* 1933; insurance policy for the *Royal Palace Hotel* of Phnom Penh, 1929. On the left page : above, facade of the *Langbian Palace* around 1930; below : building of the *Royal Palace Hotel* in Phnom Penh about which Somerset Maugham had mixed feelings : ''The hotel is large, dirty and pretentious, and there is a terrace outside it where the merchants and the innumerable functionaries may take an aperitif and for a moment forget that they are not in France.''

"The *jinrikshas* took us up a steep slope through peaceful streets to the top of Boa Vista, where a hotel of the same name is situated. It is one of the best, if not the best, of its kind in the Far East. The rooms have balconies overlooking the sea. The waves break on the rocks on which the house has been built; from the garden comes the sweet fragrance of orange blossoms." Cécile de Rodt, 1904.

The *Boa Vista Hotel* was opened in 1870 by Captain Clarke and it remained his property until 1901 when he decided to sell it. Through the good offices of the French Consul in Canton, he received an offer from the Governor General of Indochina who wanted to open a sanatorium for French soldiers exhausted by the climate. The place had the reputation of being healthy and it would be less expensive to get the sick to recuperate there than to send them back home. A minor political scandal ensued. Alarmed at this French intrusion, the British Government urged the Government of Macao to prevent the deal from going through : the whole area was expropriated and Captain Clarke's property was foisted on a charitable institution - the Santa Casa. Officially, it was supposed to have been transformed into a hospital, but nothing was ever done to bring this about. In 1903, a William Farmer tried to buy it, but changed his mind and bought the *Macao Hotel* instead. In the following years the *Boa Vista* was successively a secondary school, a camp for Portuguese refugees from Shanghai or Hong Kong when the Japanese occupied these places, and finally British Army headquarters 1947. It was only after the war that it became a hotel again under the name of *Bela Vista*.

Above : The *Macao Hotel* in the 1930s. Below : baggage label of the *Hotel Riviera* (formerly *Macao Hotel*) in the 1930s. On the left page : terrace and main staircase of the *Bela Vista*, 1985.

MEZZANINE
FLOOR.

ROSS SE

Palmer Turner.
architect
Aug. 1922

The *Peninsula* was officially inaugurated on 11 December 1928. The opening had been expected for the last four years and repeatedly delayed, so that the hotel had become something of a myth. The whole population of Hong Kong awaited the festivities with enthusiasm and curiosity. When it opened, an enormous crowd rushed into the monumental building, shining with gold. The *Daily Press* reported the event : "The hotel was thronged with visitors who were permitted to wander at will and see for themselves all its wonders, and there were exclamations of surprise and admiration to be heard on every side. Particularly piquant was an observation on the lips of an American woman : 'It makes me feel like a million dollars. I'd feel rich here even if I hadn't a dime in my bag.' That was the general impression. Some of the visitors felt the magnificence a trifle overpowering but others were wholehearted in their admiration. Refreshments were served on both the first and sixth floors and several gentlemen were seen to be availing themselves of the services of the newly opened barber's shop."

Above : cover of a contemporary publicity pamphlet mentioning that, since 1970, a fleet of chauffeur-driven Rolls-Royces is at the disposal of the *Peninsula's* guests. Below : facade of the hotel in 1927, a year before it was inaugurated. On the left page : elevation of the hotel by Palmer & Turner, the firm which designed the building.

Above : members of the managing staff having their picture
taken in front of the *Peninsula*,
1928. Facing page : 1 - the *Hong
Kong Hotel*, 1869; 2 - publicity
material, 1943 : during the Japanese occupation the hotel's name
was changed into *Toa Hotel*; 3
-British soldiers in the *Peninsula*
in 1927; the occupation by British
troops delayed its inauguration
and it had to be renovated after
their departure. On the right
page : cake baked for the inauguration of the new offices of the
Hong Kong and Shanghaï Ban-
king Corporation, *Hong Kong
Hotel*, 1930; Leo Gaddi (on right)
who began as a cook at the *Hong
Kong Hotel* became Manager of
the *Peninsula* in 1948.

香港 東亜ホテル 九龍

2

3

Above : the hotel and the beach of Repulse Bay in the 1930s. Facing page : the main building of the *Repulse Bay Hotel* in the 1920s. The words "Hong Kong Hotel" on the pediment were never used but are a reminder that the building was financed by the Hong Kong Hotel Co.

T he Bund, a sort of Chinese Manhattan built along the river Huang-P'u, was the shop window of Western imperialism. Banks and great hotels were built there in the 1930s and have remained part of the urban landscape. Today, the Bund is still Shanghai's commercial centre and fashionable promenade.
Above : the Bund in 1935; on the right, the pyramidal roof of the *Peace Hotel* (formerly the *Cathay*). On the previous pages : the Bund in the 1970s : on the left, the *Peace Hotel* and on the right the *Shanghai Mansions*. Below : facade of the *Astor House,* built around 1910 and situated behind the *Shanghai Mansions.* On the left page : above, at the corner of the Bund and Nanking Street, the *Central Hotel,* in 1900; below, the dining room of the *Palace Hotel* built in 1907, on the site of the *Central Hotel.* The *Palace Hotel* is now under the same management as the *Peace Hotel* which was built in 1931 on the opposite side of Nanking Street.

THE NEW SASSOON HOUSE
SHANGHAI
PALMER & TURNER · ARCHITECTS · SHANGHAI

I n the 1930s, the *Cathay Hotel,* then brand new, was the meeting place for everybody who counted in Shanghai, or at any rate for the members of the Western elite who lived in the foreign concessions. There were no Chinese except for a host of servants. It was possible to live there as if in Paris or London, removed from Shanghai's dark lanes, its underworld and its plots : "You can buy an electric razor, or a French dinner, or a well-cut suit. You can dance at the Tower Restaurant on the roof of the *Cathay Hotel,* and gossip with Freddy Kaufmann, its charming manager, about the European aristocracy or pre-Hitler Berlin…'' W.H. Auden/Christopher Isherwood, 1938.
Above : facade of the *Peace Hotel.* On the left page : facade of the *New Sassoon House (Cathay Hotel)* designed by Palmer and Turner in 1930.

H ow does one escape from fable, from allegory, on arriving in Shanghai...And why should one wish to escape from it ? Isn't it better to be carried away by these idealized representations of our most secret dreams and start getting to know Shanghai...by drinking a cup of powdered coffee at the bar of the *Cathay Hotel* where Marlene Dietrich occupied suite 441...Nothing has changed in this temple of modern style and the Lalique wall lamps shed as ungenerously as before a light conducive to confidences. Yet there is something wrong. In their eagerness to copy the West, the iconoclasts managing the place have stuck against the Bar, which would fetch a high price at a Drouot auction, a gigantic fizzy drink machine." Gérard Guegan, *Le Matin,* 1987.

Above : pathetic New Year's Eve celebration at the *Peace Hotel* (former *Cathay*), 1980. On the right page : interior of the hotel as it is today, 1-2-3 and 4 - "Crane Longevity Hall", "Farthest-Heaven Hall" and "Dragon-Phoenix Hall", four of the eight reception and banquet halls ; 5 - the Chinese Suite ; 6 - lounge opening on to the "Peace Hall".

The *Shanghai Mansions* (formerly *Broadway Mansions*) in the 1970s; the words "Long Live Mao" in neon can be seen above the hotel. It was on the top of this imposing and beautifully situated building that, on 27 March 1949, the Red Flag was hoisted for the first time. It was here, too, on the eighteenth floor terrace, that war correspondants of the great international periodicals were able to observe and discuss - with the inevitable glass of whisky in their hands - the clashes between the Nationalist and Communist forces before the People's Republic of China was established six month later (1 October 1949). On the right page : above, the *Broadway Mansions,* 1935 and below, publicity material of the 1930s for the *Park Hotel* (now *International Hotel* or *Guoji*).

The *Park Hotel* can be partly identified as the model of the "Shanghai Hotel" in a novel by Vicky Baum published in 1939. The author describes a luxurious place patronised by as elegant a crowd as the *Cathay* from which she probably also drew her inspiration.

The

PARK HOTEL

SHANGHAI

At Bubbling Well Road
Overlooking the Race Course

The Newest and Most Modern Hotel
in the Far East

Air Conditioned Lounge and Dining Room

RATES

American Plan :

Single Rooms From . $ 12.00
Double Rooms From . $ 22.00

*Pilgrims are welcome to the Sightseeing Gallery
on the 21st floor, which offers a most impressive
panoramic view of Shanghai.*

Telephone : 91010   Max Schibler, Manager

Operated by the International Hotels, Ltd.

Tientsin, Astorhouse Hotel

T ien-tsin, "The capital's gate to the sea", was coveted by the Western powers as early as 1858. Control of this city situated not far from Peking would enable them to put pressure on the Imperial Government. A great number of foreign concessions were established there and this led to the building of hotels for people travelling on business. A few of them still exist, such as the *Astor House Hotel* (shown above at the beginning of the century) which has become the *Tianjin*. Below : baggage label of the *Nanking Hotel*, Nanking, in the 1930s. On the right page : baggage label of the *Grand Hôtel des Wagons-Lits* (which the CIWL ceased to manage in 1905). The Japanese elite become accustomed to Western ways in this hotel situated in the diplomatic enclave bordering the Jade Canal. The *North China Daily Mail* "was the first to reveal to its readers that the *Wagons-Lit Hotel* of Peking was the official purveyor of western products to the Imperial Palace. These were served at the table of the Dowager Empress where meals were eaten with knives and forks imported directly from Sheffield, England." (Brian Power). Today there is a restaurant in the half-ruined building of the *Grand Hôtel des Wagons-Lits*.

GRAND HOTEL DES
WAGONS LITS
PEKIN

HONGKONG & SHANGHAI HOTELS, LTD.

The *Grand Hôtel de Pékin* was opened in 1900. The same year, a secret society called the Fists of Righteous Harmony, which opposed the Western presence in China, besieged the diplomatic enclave in Peking. The dramatic and bloody incidents that followed became known as the Boxer Rebellion. Designed for foreign guests, the new hotel symbolized the intrusion of the West in China and it was feared that it would be one of the main targets of the rebels. Situated on the outskirts of the Legation Quarter, it was in a vulnerable position and could not resist a siege. The Swiss manager, Mr Chamot, asked his guests to vacate the hotel and offered to lodge them in a pavilion belonging to the British Legation. Until the arrival of the international expeditionary force, Chamot did everything he could to make them comfortable, and his French chef, showing great imagination, served them pony and horse meat under many guises.

Above : *The Grand Hôtel de Pékin* around 1920; this was built in 1917 and replaced the earlier one. It still exists but is now part of a compound comprising a wing on the western side built in 1956 and another on the eastern side built in 1974. Below : baggage label of the *Grand Hôtel de Pékin,* 1930. On the left page : main staircase, 1920. On the following pages : on the left, main lounge; on the right, a bedroom and a private drawing room, 1920.

日本の館

T he most beautiful buildings of Nara, the ancient capital of Imperial Japan, are dispersed in the vast grounds of a huge garden teeming with sacred deer - the least shy of animals. There, on a little mound, the *Nara Hotel* was built. The beauty of the site is enough to justify the fame of this hotel; from its windows the guest can see Mount Wakakusa, the marvellous Todaiji pagoda - which is supposed to be the oldest wooden building in the world - or the Kofukuji pagoda. The idea of building this hotel developed after the Treaty of Portsmouth ended the Russo-Japanese war. The interest of the Europeans was aroused by this event and Japan experienced a sudden flow of tourists. The initiative came from the Government, and the building was constructed under the supervision of the National Company of Japanese Railways. The *Nara Hotel* opened in 1909, and the cost of construction, intended to symbolize Japanese prestige, was seven times the original estimate.

Above : north facade of the *Nara Hotel,* 1930. Below : general view of the buildings, 1980s. On the left page : above, porch of the main entrance around 1950; below, Emperor Hirohito and the Empress during their stay at the *Nara Hotel* in May 1981. On the previous pages : inset, European-style buildings facing the sea with, on the right, the *Hiago Hotel,* Kobe, 1890; general view of Kobe harbour in the 1920s with, in the background, the *Oriental Hotel* where Kipling stayed. He retained a happy memory of the food : "Let me sing the praises of the excellent M. Begeux, proprietor of the *Oriental Hotel,* upon whom be peace. This is a house where you can dine...I have eaten curries of the rarest at the *Oriental* of Penang. The turtle steaks of *Raffles* at Singapore still live in my regretful memory, and they gave me chicken liver and suckling pig in the *Victoria* at Hong Kong which I shall always extol. But the *Oriental* at Kobe was better than all three." *From Sea to Sea*, 1899.

A group of American actors arrive at the *Nara Hotel,* among them, <u>above</u>, Marlon Brando and Glenn Ford, 1954. <u>On the left page</u> : ''the Imperial Suite'' of the *Nara* (notice the slippers prepared at the foot of the bed, a common practice in Japanese hotels) and the main lounge, 1930s.

<u>On the following pages</u> : the *Fujiya Hotel,* Miyanoshita, a town in the Hakone region, before the 1923 earthquake. In 1871, for the first time in the history of Japan, a diplomatic mission - the Iwakura mission - was sent to visit Europe and the United States. One of the passengers on the ship by which they travelled was a young man, Sennosuke Yamaguchi. He stayed abroad for three years and came back obsessed by the idea of setting up a Westernized hotel. Looking around for a suitable spot he found, in a region full of warm springs and bubbling waterfalls, a small inn in the town of Miyanoshita. He renamed it *Fujiya Hotel* and opened it in 1878. In the beginning of the century, the hotel acquired an international reputation and was patronized by foreign guests on official visits to Japan. Among these have been members of a German delegation attending the funeral of Emperor Meiji; the Duke of Gloucester who came to bestow the Order of the Garter on Emperor Hirohito; the royal family of Sweden, and well-known American figures from General Eisenhower to John Foster Dulles and General Ridgway, and of course General MacArthur whose name is to be found in the registers of all the great hotels of Japan. But the most regular guest was Emperor Hirohito who has happy memories of the *Fujiya*. It was there, when he was still Crown Prince, that he discovered the pleasures of golf on the course built in 1917. He tried his hand at this occidental game every year until 1921 when, having become Emperor and feeling the weight of his divine ancestry, he had to give up such frivolous pursuits.

The *Grand* is the semi or cottage *Grand* really, but you had better go there unless a friend tells you of a better. A long course of good luck has spoiled me for even average hotels. They are too fine and large as the *Grand,* and they don't always live up to their grandeur; unlimited electric bells, but no one in particular to answer them; printed menu, but the firstcomers eat all the nice things, and so forth. Nonetheless, there are points about the *Grand* not to be despised.'' Rudyard Kipling, *From Sea to Sea,* 1895.

Until the 19th century the *Grand* remained modest and only grew to be a hotel of international repute in 1920 when prosperity came to Yokohama.

Above : the seaside facade of the *Yokohama Grand Hotel* in 1880 and the facade of the *New Grand* facing the garden in the 1930s.

Facing page : a ''runner'' attached to the *Grand Hotel,* accompanying a guest for a walk in the streets of Yokohama; the year is 1920 and the time probably spring, as cherry and plum trees are in bloom.

The *Grand* of Yokohama opened in September 1873. It was a two-storied building facing the sea and had thirty rooms, a restaurant and a library. It was completely destroyed in the great earthquake of 1923 which killed 150,000 people. A young architect, Jin Watanabe, designed the new building on larger (ninety-four rooms) and more luxurious lines. It opened in 1927. The main hall, on the first floor, was the showpiece. Supported by massive wooden pillars, it was decorated with marble imported from Italy and was furnished in the Western style. The *New Grand* became fashionable and knew some good years until the war. "Fantastic days" recalls Yasunori Yamagaki who has remained with the staff and is now its senior member. He had his photograph taken with the celebrities of the time, rich Americans, baseball champions and film stars of the silent era : Mary Pickford, Douglas Fairbanks, Charlie Chaplin. In 1940 the *New Grand* was taken over by the military and occupied for twelve years, the Japanese being supplanted by the Americans at the end of the war. When MacArthur landed without warning, the *New Grand* was in a poor state with its walls full of cracks. Yet it was the only hotel still open in the heavily bombed town. The awed cook managed to serve the General a steak that the latter's staff feared might be poisoned, but MacArthur ate it calmly. In 1952 the hotel was at last freed from military occupation but it had to be entirely renovated. The younger members of the staff were entrusted with the task of cleaning the walls and they remember it to this day.

<u>Above</u> : top, photographs of the main hall; bottom, crockery of the *New Grand* and newspaper rack, 1987. <u>On the left page</u> : Mr Suzuki, public relations officer, and Yasunori Yamagaki, veteran of the *New Grand*.

I t is common practice in Japan for weddings to take place in hotels which not only arrange for the receptions, banquets and balls but also provide accommodation for guests who come from afar to congratulate the couple. This practice which provides a regular source of income for hotels dates back to the time when traditional inns served the same purpose. More than three hundred weddings per year take place at the *New Grand* these days. The hotel provides for everything and presents its customers with a wide choice of invitation cards and menus delicately decorated. It is seldom that one can stay in a Japanese hotel even for a day without running into a gay wedding party led by a young man in tails and a young woman in kimono or white wedding dress.

Above : wedding of an American couple living in Japan, ballroom of the *New Grand,* 1930s. Below : newlywed couple, photograph taken by the hotel photographer, 1935. On the right page : the newlywed couple and family taken in the ballroom (above), in the inner courtyard of the *New Grand* (below), 1930s.

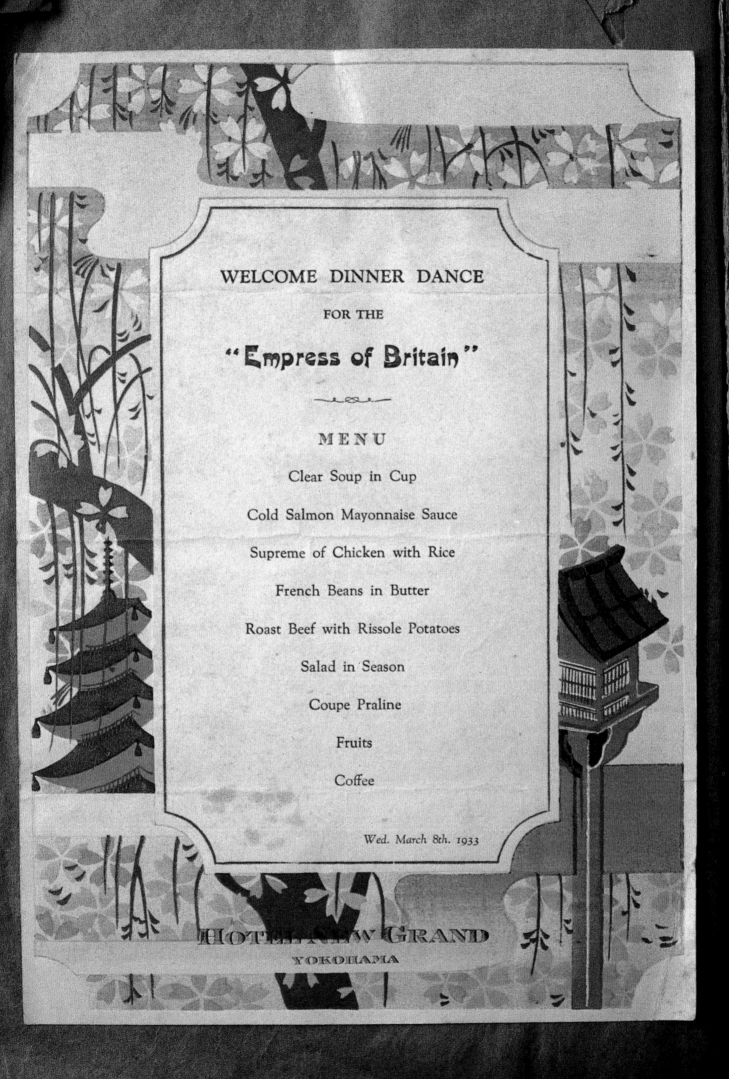

WELCOME DINNER DANCE

FOR THE

"Empress of Britain"

MENU

Clear Soup in Cup

Cold Salmon Mayonnaise Sauce

Supreme of Chicken with Rice

French Beans in Butter

Roast Beef with Rissole Potatoes

Salad in Season

Coupe Praline

Fruits

Coffee

Wed. March 8th. 1933

HOTEL NEW GRAND

YOKOHAMA

Before the war, even apart from wedding ceremonies, the Yokohama *New Grand* was the place to celebrate. Parties for the national days of other countries, such as American Independence Day or Bastille Day, Christmas and New Year's Eve, when the gaiety went on until dawn, or any other occasion when celebration was indicated, were all held here. Asked what is his happiest memory of his sixty years' service in the hotel, Mr Yasunori Yamagaki remembers the famous New Year's Eves : at midnight the lights went off suddenly in the ballroom and the guests could kiss their elegant companions…just that once in the whole year! Great festivities also greeted the arrival of the big ships from Europe and America. They ended with fireworks that lit up the bay to the applause of crowds watching from the restaurant.
<u>Above</u> : the ballroom with a banquet in progress, 1930s. <u>Below</u> : yet another newlywed couple. <u>On the left page</u> : menu of a dinner-dance given on the occasion of the arrival of the "Empress of Britain", 1933.

The *Gajoen* opened in Tokyo in the Meguro Ku district at the beginning of the 1930s as a restaurant serving Chinese food. The premises - a large building surrounded, Japanese style, by a labyrinthine garden - soon became too small. A new multi-storey wing was built opposite the original one, in a mixture of local and Western styles. It became a "house of banquets" with a great number of dining rooms of various sizes which, with the help of sliding doors, could be made bigger or smaller according to the number of guests. The then manager, Mr Hosokawa, is remembered for his generosity and his love of art. Many young artists frequented his place and, often finding themselves short of funds, paid their bill by contributing an original work to the decoration of the establishment. In the 1940s, when the building was transformed into a hotel, it was found to be crammed with them : murals, ceilings decorated with human figures or floral patterns, great ornamented screens. But the pride of the *Gajoen* is its lift : the cabin made of brightly-coloured lacquer decorated with mother of pearl and metal inlays is in the shape of a group of young girls. There is no more charming hotel in the whole of Tokyo. The best place to stay is a corner room in the old wing. Two big windows make up two of the walls and, beyond the garden, these overlook the huge jumbled mass of Tokyo.

Above : The facade of the *Gajoen* as it is today. Below : patterns painted in the 1930s on the ceiling of a corridor in the old wing. On the right page : passage leading to the old wing, 1987. On the following pages : the great banquet hall, 1987.

I n 1929 Prince Li, a Korean nobleman, had a palace built in Tokyo where he entertained his guests when visiting the Japanese capital. It withstood the great earthquake and was converted into a hotel in 1957. Competition was extensive in this central part of Tokyo - Chiyoda Ku - where ultra-modern hotels were built in great numbers. In 1983, an enormous tower containing 761 rooms and 9 restaurants was added to the *Akasaka Prince Hotel* and the old residence of the Korean Prince became an annexe. For reasons of security (Japanese rules are very strict, especially as regards fire risks), it is forbidden for guests to be put up there. The rooms have been transformed into private lounges and dining rooms. Diners gather in Princesse Li's green room. The French food served in the first floor restaurant is excellent. Cocktail parties and of course weddings also take place there.

<u>Above</u> : the *Akasaka Prince Hotel,* the old building and the new tower. <u>On the right page</u> : <u>above</u>, a ground floor drawing room, 1987; <u>below</u>, the first floor restaurant, details, 1987.

FIRST STUDY
OF THE BUILDING
APPROVED 1913-

IMPER

TOK

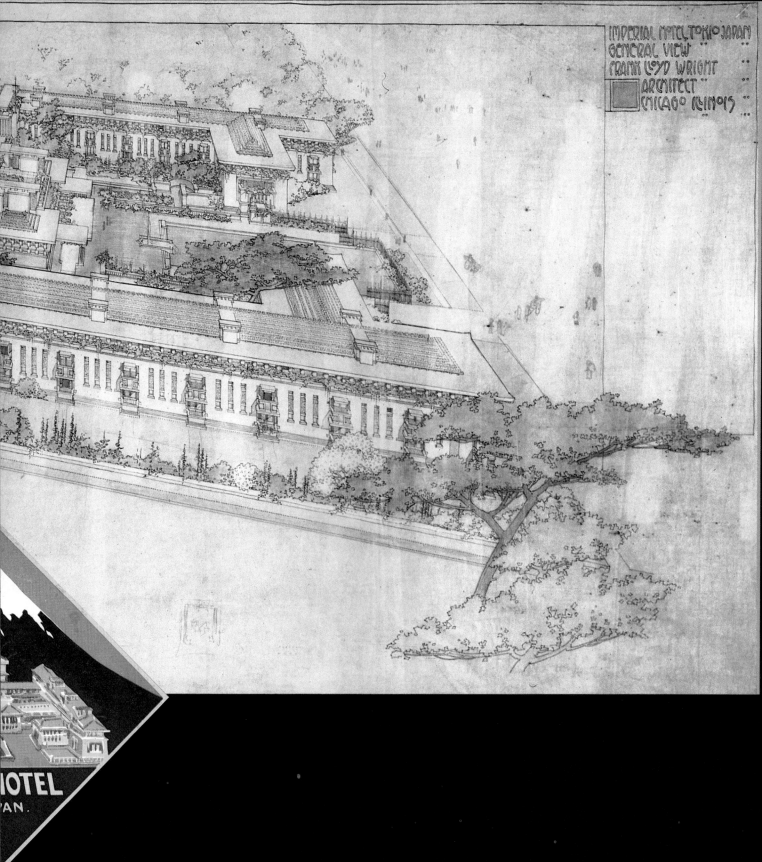

IMPERIAL HOTEL TOKIO JAPAN
GENERAL VIEW "
FRANK LLOYD WRIGHT "
ARCHITECT "
CHICAGO ILLINOIS "

HOTEL
PAN.

F rank Lloyd Wright was an exceptional man, one of the rare artists of his time to have resisted the "international style." He designed and supervised the construction of the *Imperial Hotel* between 1915 and 1922 at the end of the first part of his professional life. By the time the building was finished, hotels had become so common and popular taste so blunted that many were disconcerted by its architecture. "The architecture and decoration give a nightmarish impression : projecting cornices, blocks of lava, concealed lighting, doors which cannot be opened, miniature furnishings; and thousands of little irregular windows which only serve to keep out the daylight. Wright's idea was apparently to create something typically Japanese; he had only just arrived in the country and was certainly on the wrong track but he made up for it afterwards in the United States when he built a number of genuine Japanese houses." John Gunther, 1951. Real-estate speculation brought about the demolition of this extraordinary complex : all that remains is the entrance hall which was reconstructed in Meiji Village.

Above : the hotel staff and, behind, on the left, Frank Lloyd Wright in the 1920s. On the left page : main lounge, detail, 1920s. On the previous pages : inset, baggage label, 1930; vista, 1913.

RETURN FROM THE ORIENT

The Pages of the Album

Hôtel Plaza, Casablanca.

Hôtel Excelsior, Casablanca.

Hôtel Majestic, Tunis.

Hôtel Bellevue, Tunis.

Palace Hotel, Algiers.

Hôtel Excelsior, Algiers.

Royal Hotel, Biskra.

Hôtel du Sahara, Biskra.

Malraux discovered the East in his youth. Those were exciting and troubled times when, as Baron Clappique would say, there were "real adventurers... real originals," such as Ferral of *Man's Fate,* who kept flocks of tropical birds, parrots and a kangaroo in his mistress's rooms at the Astor House of Shanghai. Malraux went East again thirty years later and found that the grand hotels had survived the metamorphosis of the past three decades: "*Raffles* has changed but the patio surrounded by rooms with their doors banging incessantly is still there"; and the "dust that sleeps" in the Cairo museum "finds its counterpart in the old *Shepheard's Hotel.*" Even when myths disintegrate, the grand hotels of the East keep, as if embalmed, the old dreams of the West.

" **S**he had the most beautiful, the most intelligent of faces, the figure of an elephant and legs like pillars." This is how Koko Mazloumian, the manager of the *Baron* in Aleppo, remembers Agatha Christie. While her archaeologist husband was carrying out excavations in the area, she finished writing *Murder on the Orient Express* sitting on the terrace of the hotel. She had started it a few years before at the *Pera Palace* in Istanbul. At that time, she had herself become the heroine of a famous mystery by disappearing for eleven days. She did not care to explain her absence. At the time of her death, a medium found a key hidden under a board of the floor of room 411 and declared it would resolve the mystery. It has not yet done so.

Somerset Maugham is a celebrity claimed by the famous hotels of Asia. Each of them asserts that he stayed in it and that it inspired him with one of his characters or the theme of one of his short stories. It all makes for good publicity; and tourists are happy to stay in a "Somerset Maugham" suite where the writer perhaps only spent one night or where he never even set foot. Does it matter? It is best, when telling the story of the grand hotels, not to try to distinguish fable from reality. *Raffles,* in the event, was probably Maugham's favourite hotel.

Grand Hôtel, Tripoli.

Grand Hôtel Abbat, Alexandria.

Bristol Hotel, Cairo.

Hôtel Beau Rivage, Alexandria.

Semiramis Hotel, Cairo.

Return from the excursion, *Mena-House*, Cairo.

Hôtel Kaminitz, Jerusalem.

Hôtel d'Europe, Jerusalem.

Grand Hôtel Victoria, Beirut.

Hotel area, Beirut.

Grand Hôtel d'Orient or *Hôtel Bassoul*, Beirut.

Hôtel Villa des Chênes, Mount Lebanon

Hôtel Allemand, Beirut.

Grand Hôtel de Palmyre, Palmyra.

Grand Hôtel de Mme Huck, Smyrna.

Grand Hôtel, Smyrna.

Hôtels Calypso and *Giacomo*, Istanbul.

Apollo Hotel, Bombay.

Hotel Continental, Calcutta.

Bristol Hotel, Colombo.

Phya Thai Palace, Bangkok.

Adelphi Hotel, Singapore.

Australian tourists, Java.

Hôtel Marinus Jansen, Eetzaal.

Grand Hôtel de Peking, Peking.

Shanghai Mansions, Shanghai.

Grand Hôtel des Wagons-Lits, Peking.

Une note d'Hôtel de Nagoya

七 六

食 会 蒼 門

S.S. "HAKOZAKI MARU"
DINNER

Hors-d'Œuvre
Variés

Consommé à la Royale

Baked Fish Shrimp Sauce
EXTRA— Sudako Kokkoka
Grenadins de Veau à la Turque
Braised Ox-tongue with Spinach
Meat Curry and Rice

Roast Leg of Mutton Mint Sauce

Potatoes—

BAY VIEW FROM LOUNGE, THE GRAND HOTEL, YOKOHAMA.

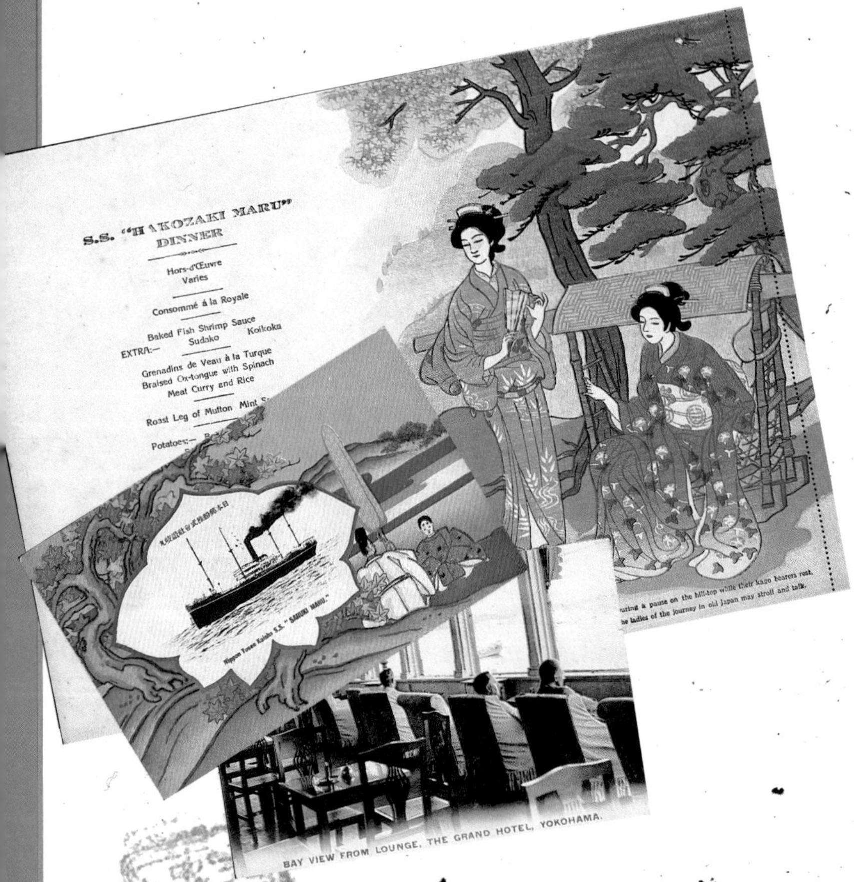

Shoumparo Hotel, Shimonoseki.

Kanaya Hotel, Nikko.

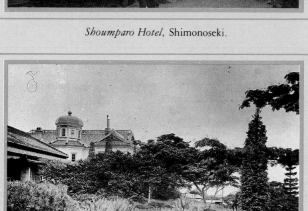

Atami Hotel, Atami.

Kyoto Hotel, Kyoto.

Osaka Hotel, Osaka.

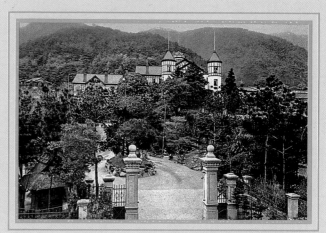

Tor Hotel, Kobe.

Tokyo Station Hotel.

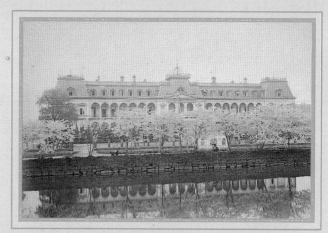

Imperial Hotel, Tokyo.

"Then night came. The
last night. I stayed a long time at my
window at the *Cecil,* contemplating
the bay, the promenade,
the sky swept from time to time by
the beam of the lighthouse.
This sight brought too many
beautiful memories to my mind. The
dark sea rolled. I packed my trunks
and went to bed''
Francis Carco, 1933.

Above : the boutonniere of pink orchids
offered by Thai Airways to the passengers
on the flight Hong-Kong-Delhi-Paris in
August 1985.

INDEX

OF HOTELS QUOTED

We chose to limit the scope of this work to hotels created or built between 1800 and 1939; however, we have allowed a few exceptions. This is the case, for instance, of the old Indian palaces which have recently been transformed into hotels. On the one hand, their repute did not permit their exclusion; on the other, the organization of these *palais d'hôtes* – aimed at occidental clients and equipped, from the beginning, with hotel-style comforts – is logically related to our subject. This is also true of certain Tokyo hotels which came later but are so characteristic of Japanese hostelry that we could not fairly deprive the reader.

In this index, page numbers in italics indicate illustrations, whereas the others refer to mention in the text.

PHOTO CREDITS

PP. 226, 227: Bettmann Archives.
PP. 228, 229: Bettmann Archives;
Yokohama *New Grand* archives.
PP. 230, 231: Marc Walter.
PP. 232-235: Yokohama *New Grand* archives.
PP. 236-239: Marc Walter.
P. 240: *Akasaka Prince Hotel* documentation.
P. 241: Marc Walter.

PP. 242-245: © G.A.
P. 246: Fouad Debbas Collection.
P. 248: Henriette Angel;
Bettmann Archives; Roger-Viollet.
P. 249: Roger-Viollet.
P. 250: Fouad Debbas Collection,
Harvard Semitic Museum; Roger-Viollet;
Bettmann Archives; M. Vandervelde.
P. 251: Fouad Debbas Collection.

P. 252: Fouad Debbas Collection;
Henriette Angel; Royal
Commonwealth Society.
P. 253: Singapore archives; Tropen
Museum; Roger-Viollet; Compagnie
Internationale des Wagons-Lits.
P. 254: Roger-Viollet.
P. 255: Henriette Angel; Royal
Commonwealth Society.

INDEX
OF TEXTS QUOTED

P. 86: *Les Belles de Tunis,* Nine
Moati, Seuil (France), 1983.
P. 97: *La Route des Indes,* Paul
Morand, Plon (France), 1936.
P. 101: *La Mort de Philae,* Pierre
Loti, 1908.
P. 109: *Sanctuaires d'Orient,* Edouard
Schuré, Librairie académique Perrin
(France), 1898.

P. 115: *The Crescent and the Cross,*
Elias Warburton, 1858.
P. 118: *Beyrouth, Viva la Muerte,*
Jules Roy, Grasset (France), 1984.
P. 125: *Lettres sur la Morée, (...) et
Constantinople,* Castellan, 2nd
edition, 1820.
P. 140: *L'Inde impudique des
maharadjahs,* V. de Golish, Laffont
(France), 1973.
P. 143: *L'Odeur de l'Inde,* Pier Paolo
Pasolini, Denoël (France), 1961.
P. 146: *From Sea to Sea,* Rudyard
Kipling, 1899.
P. 180: *La vie en Malaisie,* W. R.
Foran, Payot (France), 1936.
P. 184: Foran, op. cit.

P. 192: *La Guerre d'Indochine II -
L'Illusion,* Lucien Bodard, Gallimard
(France).
P. 197: *Voyage d'une Suissesse
autour du monde,* Cécile de Rodt,
Zahn (Switzerland), 1904.
P. 209 : *Journey to a War,* W. H.
Auden/Christopher Isherwood, 1938.
P. 214: *Le dernier fils du ciel,
1906-1967,* Brian Power, Balland
(France), 1986.
P. 222: Kipling, op. cit.
P. 229: Kipling, op. cit.
P. 245: *L'énigme MacArthur,* John
Gunther, Gallimard (France), 1951.
P. 256: *Palace Egypte,* Francis Carco,
Albin Michel (France), 1933.

ACKNOWLEDGMENTS

We wish first of all to thank all the hotels which kindly furnished us with documentation and information without which this book would not have been possible, in particular: the *Akasaka Prince Hotel,* the *American Colony,* the *Baron* (and Mr Koko Mazloumian), the Macao *Bela Vista,* the *Cairo Marriott Hotel,* the Penang *Eastern & Oriental,* the *Gajoen* (and Mr Kato), the *Galle Face,* the *Goodwood Park Hotel,* the *Grand Hôtel de Pékin,* the *King David,* the *Mamounia,* the *Manila,* the Yokohama *New Grand,* the Bangkok *Oriental,* the Shanghai *Peace Hotel,* the *Peninsula,* the *Pera Palace,* the *Raffles,* the *Taj* (and Mme Umaima Mulla-Feroze) and the *Umaid Bhawan* (and the Maharajah of Jodhpur).

In addition, our thanks to all the museums, archives and various firms which were willing to aid our research, especially: the Penang Museum, the Tropen Museum of Amsterdam, the Singapore Archives, the Macao Tourist Office, the Algerian National Tourist Office, the Tunisian Hotel Federation, the Oberoi chain, the Compagnie des Wagons-Lits and the Palmer & Turner (Hong Kong).

Our gratitude extends to those collectors kind enough to share certain documents and sometimes even further our research. Extremely valuable was the assistance of: Catherine Barret, Charles Bastin and J. Evrard, Pascal Boissel, Fouad Debbas and V. Denis Vandervelde.

Our thanks also to those who, out of friendship, furnished complementary information or photographs: Robert Arndt, editor-in-chief of *Aramco* magazine, John Carswell, Jean Dethier, Sylvie Forbin of the French embassy in Beijing, Mr Franchini and Mr Sarkies.

Finally, we would like to thank Mr Plouseau, director of the Paris *Claridge-Bellman,* who personally put us in contact with the hotel chains; and Mme Bauthéac whose efficient collaboration considerably enriched the present book.